sewing vintage aprons

by denise clason

DEDICATION

This book is dedicated to four very important and influential women in my life, all of whom inspired me to find my creative and artistic side. My mother, Ailene; my maternal grandmother, Sadie; my paternal grandmother, Evelyn; and last but not least, my daughter, Erin. Some of the aprons are named after them. They are, and will always be, my inspiration.

ACKNOWLEDGEMENTS

I would like to thank All-American Crafts for the opportunity to write *Sewing Vintage Aprons*. Thank you to Pam Mostek for her interest in publishing my book idea! Thank you to Sue Harvey for her great editing skills. Thank you to Kelly Albertson for the design and beautiful artistry of *Sewing Vintage Aprons*. Thank you to Carol Newman for her "eye" while taking photos for my book. A big thank you to all who contributed to the look and feel of this book! *Sewing Vintage Aprons* is beautiful because of all of you! Readers … please enjoy… it was created for you!

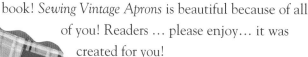

Published by

All American Crafts, Inc.
7 Waterloo Road
Stanhope, NJ 07874
www.allamericancrafts.com

Publisher | **Jerry Cohen**

Chief Executive Officer | **Darren Cohen**

Product Development
Director | **Brett Cohen**

Editor | **Sue Harvey**

Art Director | **Kelly Albertson**

Photography | **Kathleen Geary**

Illustrations | **Rory Byra**

Product Development
Manager | **Pamela Mostek**

Vice President/Quilting Advertising
& Marketing | **Carol Newman**

Printed in China
©2010 Denise Clason
ISBN: 978-0-9819762-7-3
Library of Congress Control
Number: 2011901564

INTRODUCTION

I have always loved aprons! I remember my mother wearing them when I was a little girl and the excitement I felt when she tied one on me to help her cook. There was something fun and sweet about wearing that big apron. I felt like a big girl and that made me feel just as experienced as my mother. Later, I believed that everything I made tasted better because I was wearing an apron. It was like magic! That magic continued as I became a mother and tied a big apron on my little children. They also felt big and special as they helped me in the kitchen. I so enjoy sharing my history and memories with my children and their children, passing memories from generation to generation. I see my daughter putting an apron on her 2-year-old son, Ryan, and how much he loves wearing it! As I worked on an apron for this book, Ryan said, "I wanna wear it." This put a big smile on grandma's face.

My grandmother Evelyn wore an apron all the time. She called it her housecoat. It was so used that it wore thin, and you could see her blouse underneath. Her housecoat was more of the "cobbler" style, with armholes and snaps or buttons to close the front and two big pockets on either side. I can see it now—such a sweet memory.

My grandmother Sadie wore half aprons most of the time but sometimes wore a full apron to protect her clothes while cooking. She loved to cook and grew a garden. Her homemade apron became part of her arms and hands as it carried produce from the garden into the house. She was adventurous and made jams, jellies, and pickles. Her bread and butter pickles were the best. She even used zucchini and watermelon rinds to make pickles. I'm grateful to have such wonderful memories.

The apron became one of my true joys in life. Even as adults, my children still enjoy cooking and working in the kitchen while they wear their aprons. And they have their favorites, too.

There is something about a vintage apron, how it looks and how it makes you feel. *Sewing Vintage Aprons* will give you that same experience. Sew an apron for yourself, your family, and friends. Bring back the nostalgia of the past—bring out the inner chef in you as you make your own memories! Get started by making an apron and then wear it while making a peach cobbler (page 43) or your family's favorite dessert! Yummm!

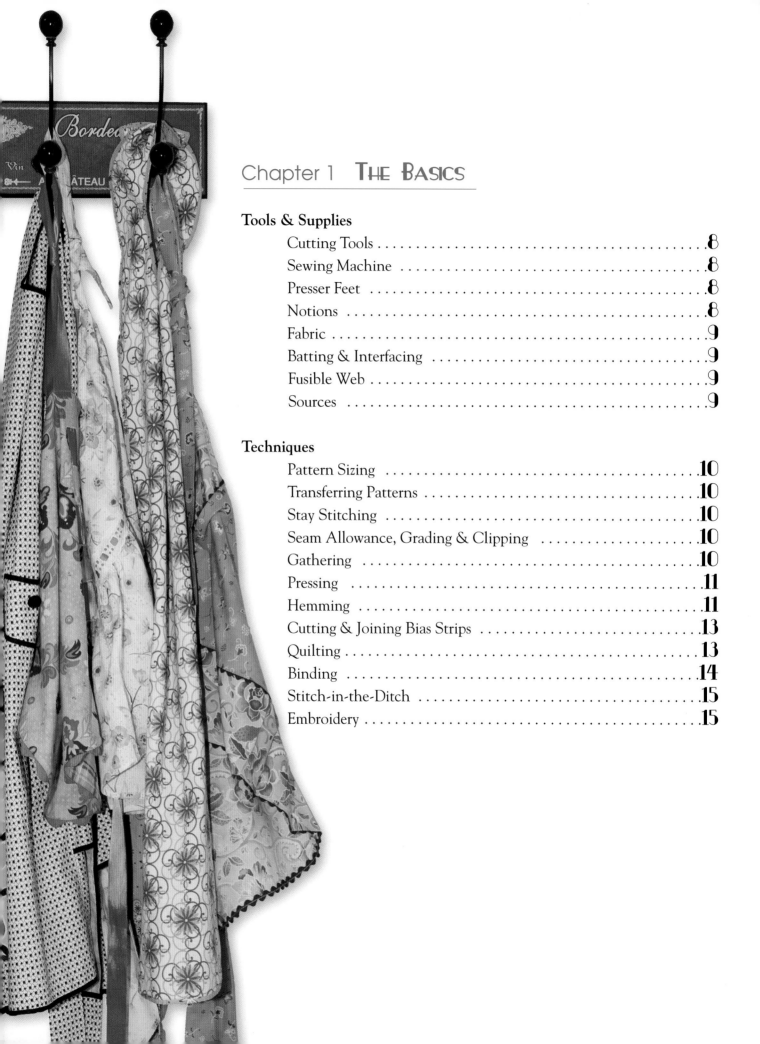

Chapter 1   THE BASICS

Tools & Supplies

Cutting Tools 8

Sewing Machine 8

Presser Feet 8

Notions 8

Fabric 9

Batting & Interfacing 9

Fusible Web 9

Sources 9

Techniques

Pattern Sizing 10

Transferring Patterns 10

Stay Stitching 10

Seam Allowance, Grading & Clipping 10

Gathering 10

Pressing 11

Hemming 11

Cutting & Joining Bias Strips 13

Quilting 13

Binding 14

Stitch-in-the-Ditch 15

Embroidery 15

Chapter 2 HALF APRONS

Minnie's Apron 18
Sadie's Apron 22
Ailene's Apron (variation of Sadie's Apron) 28
Annie's Apron 32
Pearl's Apron 36
Evelyn's Apron 40

Chapter 3 FULL APRONS

Erin's Apron 46
Evie's Apron 50
Lizzie's Apron 54
Jane's Apron 58
Grace's Apron 62

Chapter 4 QUILTED PROJECTS

Yo-Yo Table Runner 70
Ruffled Placemats 74
Ruffled Oven Mitts 76
Circle Oven Mitts 78

About the Author 80

THE BASICS
Chapter 1

A. Cutting Tools

You'll be using several different types of cutting tools. I prefer Olfa rotary cutters and mats; they have always been my favorite. Select the variety that works best for you. For the projects in this book, I recommend a 3½" x 24" ruler. I also prefer using a 24" x 36" mat. A larger mat will give you plenty of room to cut out your pieces.

For larger pattern pieces, I use a cutting board that is made of cardboard. It measures approximately 33" x 56" and folds up when not in use. I lay it on top of my kitchen table and cut away. I just love this board for all my layouts and cutting.

You'll also need a good pair of 8" dressmaking shears for cutting and trimming. I absolutely love Gingher shears. They are a little more expensive, so I buy them on sale! They surpass all other brands when I need to cut several layers of fabric and trim in tight places.

B. Sewing Machine

Make sure that your sewing machine is in tip-top shape. Have it oiled and cleaned prior to use so that it gives you the best performance. I change my needle with each new project (about 8 hours of sewing time). I used Schmetz 80-12 Universal needles for the projects in this book. If you are using a heavier fabric, use a heavier needle, such as 90-14.

C. Presser Feet

You'll need to use several different types of presser feet for projects in this book. Each project will give you a list of feet you'll need. Some of these feet are: walking foot, darning foot, cording or tricot foot (for making piping), ¼" quilting foot, embroidery foot (for machines that can embroider), and an all-purpose foot. You'll find that using the right foot will give you the best performance and result.

D. Notions

You'll need a variety of notions to make the projects in this book. Here are some of my tried-and-true favorites.

Grip Enhancer: A grip enhancer is wonderful for craftwork where your hands need "traction." I use LickityGrip. It is great for machine quilting; it helps your fingertips grip the project, which reduces hand and arm fatigue. I use it for piecing and holding fabrics together. It is also nice for threading a needle.

Anti-Fray Solution: Keep ribbons and trim looking picture perfect by using this product to prevent fraying. It is also great for keeping seam ends and embroidery stitches from raveling. I prefer Fray Check by Prym Consumer USA; it dries clear—and won't wash out!

Spray Sizing: I recommend using sizing while making the aprons in this book and for a final press when they are completed. This step will give the apron a "true" vintage look and feel. It was very popular to iron aprons and almost all clothing with starch years ago! You may surprise yourself and decide to iron your aprons after each wash, the crispness and clean look makes it look new. You'll feel like a chef when you're wearing your crisp apron!

Thread: You will need 300-yard spools of thread for the projects in this book. Some of the projects in this book require you to purchase a few colors. Select threads that match your fabrics. Pick a color that is just slightly darker than the background of your print. This will make your sewing look professional. For stitching-in-the-ditch I use a 50-weight thread, such as Aurifil. This thread practically disappears in the seams, it's great!

Basting Products: When it comes to basting, use thread, pins, or temporary spray adhesives; there are a variety of products on the market to fit your needs. Find the method that works best for you. I prefer Sulky KK2000 Temporary Spray Adhesive; it really speeds up basting. They have a new "green" product with a green cap.

Stiletto Tool: A stiletto is a "must-have" tool. It makes it so much easier to work with fabric while you are sewing, especially in tight spaces. Use it to adjust and hold your fabric when stitching straight or curved seams, or when positioning or sewing trims or embellishments. It is great for keeping your bias tape and apron fabrics together while sewing. I actually use my seam ripper to do all of the above. Mine is magnetic and helps me slide my pins out and lifts them up to place back into my pincushion.

Yo-Yo Maker: One of the projects in this book calls for yo-yos. I found them so easy to make with a yo-yo maker by Clover! Use the 1¾" yo-yo maker and follow the manufacturer's instructions—you can't go wrong! I'm not afraid to make them anymore. They turn out perfect every time.

Bias Tape Maker: You may decide to make your own double-fold bias tape. I found a tool that makes this very easy—a ½" bias tape maker. All you need is a 1"-wide bias strip, your iron, and some spray sizing!

Marking Tools: I use chalk pencils in white, silver or yellow to transfer pattern marks to the fabric pieces. Use

SUPPLIES

the lightest color that will still show on the fabric. Do not press over a chalk mark that is on the right side of a project. The heat from the iron may set the color so that it cannot be removed. Use a dry toothbrush or damp cloth to remove chalk marks.

E. Fabric

Choosing fabric is one of my favorite things to do! I love putting combinations together. The best and most enjoyable way to select fabrics is to dig in and surround yourself with colors and patterns. Don't be shy; take the bolts from the shelves and unroll them and lay them on top of other fabrics. Look at the patterns and see how the colors blend or contrast with each other. Some of the projects, such as Evelyn's Apron on page 40, work best when there is a contrast in the prints. The pocket really works when it is made in a complementary color (colors that are opposites on the color wheel, such as red and green, or variations of those colors).

All of the aprons in this book use 100% cotton fabric. It is up to you to choose the weight of the fabric, but some of the aprons are not suitable for heavier fabrics, such as those that have ruffles or gathers. Flat or straight aprons, such as Minne's Apron on page 18 and Evie's Apron on page 50, can handle a heavier "decorator" fabric. Be sure to choose fabric that is machine washable.

F. Batting & Interfacing

Batting and interfacing help to support and structure projects in this book. I recommend using 100% cotton batting for best results. I prefer Warm & Natural needle-punched batting by The Warm Company. It is absolutely my favorite. You'll also be using another product by The Warm Company called Insul-Bright. It is made for heat resistance and used in the oven mitts, placemats and table runner to protect your hands and table. When using it for the oven mitts, combine it with a layer of Warm & Natural batting. Instructions for this are given in each project.

I prefer to use lightweight iron-on woven interfacing. It is so much more pliable than non-woven interfacing and works nicely with woven fabric. It is sometimes hard to find, so you may need to ask for it.

G. Fusible Web

I use Steam-A-Seam 2 by The Warm Company whenever I need something secured. It can replace hand stitching, especially in tight places. I use it to secure the waistband before I topstitch and to hold facings secure. I also use it for hemming. I used ¼" wide Steam-A-Seam 2 for the projects in this book.

H. Sources

I know it can be frustrating to search for supplies suggested for use in a pattern and have no luck finding them. I've mentioned many of my favorite tools and supplies throughout this section. Here is information to help you locate them:

Aurifil Thread
50-weight thread
www.aurifil.com/web

Clover Needlecraft Inc.
Yo-Yo Maker, D-rings, and Bias Tape Maker
www.clover-usa.com

Henry Glass Fabrics
Opulence collection by Brenda Pinnick
(used to make the Yo-Yo Table Runner)
www.henryglassfabrics.com

Pellon
Iron-on interfacing
www.pellonideas.com

Prym Consumer USA
Fray Check
www.dritz.com

Simplicity
Bias Tape Maker
www.simplicity.com

Sulky of America
Machine Embroidery Thread, KK2000 Temporary Spray Adhesive, and Tear Away Stabilizer
www.sulky.com

The Warm Company
Warm & Natural, Insul-bright, Steam-A-Seam 2
www.warmcompany.com

Wimpole Street
Tea towel
www.wimpolestreet.com

Wrights
Rick Rack, Double fold Bias Tape, Maxi-Piping, and Ribbon
www.ezquilt.com

A. Pattern Sizing

Most of the patterns in this book are designed for all sizes, but if you need to shorten the area between the shoulder and the waist, I have marked a line on the pattern piece for the best area to do so. Remember that when you cut or fold the area to shorten you are taking away double the distance. If you fold the area by ½" you are taking out 1" of length. This is VERY important to remember, you definitely don't want to cut something too short!

In addition, if you think you want to make the pattern a little narrower in the front, you can move the fold line just a little, over the fold of the fabric, to make it narrower. Remember you will also be taking away double the distance. So, if you move the fold over a ½", you are taking out 1" of width.

B. Transferring Patterns

The patterns in this book are full size and printed on paper. They are on the pullout sheets in the back of the book. Use tissue paper and trace your patterns with a soft pencil. You can then use a felt pen to darken the lines. Transfer ALL markings onto the tissue paper as if it were the actual pattern because it will become your pattern! Save the original patterns in the book and refer back to your tissue paper for making additional aprons. The pocket patterns and facing patterns when necessary are on the apron patterns and will need to be transferred separately from the apron. **Note:** *Use iron-on interfacing or stabilizer to strengthen your tissue paper patterns for multiple uses.*

Some of the projects in the book do not use patterns to cut the pieces, or use patterns for only some of the pieces. The instructions give you measurements to cut these pieces with scissors or rotary cutting tools.

C. Stay Stitching

Stay stitching is a great method when you need to secure your fabric and keep it from stretching while you sew.

1. Press edges with sizing.

2. Using 10-12 stitches per inch, sew close to the seam line within the seam allowance to secure the fabric and keep it from stretching out of shape.

D. Seam Allowance, Grading & Clipping

The seam allowances in this book are 1/4", unless otherwise mentioned. I use my ¼" quilting foot for most of my sewing to keep my seam allowances accurate. I switch to an all-purpose foot when I need to zigzag a seam.

Grading and clipping are methods of "slimming" seam allowances to make them smooth and to remove thickness.

Seam Allowances: If the seam allowance is wider than ¼", trim it to ¼" with a good pair of shears.
Grading: Cut one layer of the seam allowance in half to reduce thickness and bulk as directed in project instructions.
Clipping: Make V-shaped cuts into the seam allowance in several places just to the stitching line, but not into it, around curves. Snip into inside corners just to the stitching line. Trim off the seam allowance at an angle on outside corners, trimming just to the stitching line.

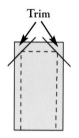 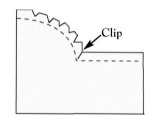

E. Gathering

All gathering stitches are 5mm in length (the longest stitch on your machine).

1. Sew the first row of stitches ⅛" from raw edge. Sew the second row of stitching ¼" from the raw edge.

2. Tie the two bobbin threads together at one end of the stitching lines. Pull the two bobbin threads at the other end of the stitching lines to make even gathers. Adjust gathers to equal proportions along the length. **Note:** *To make it easier to spread gathers evenly across an area, divide fabric into four sections and then gather.*

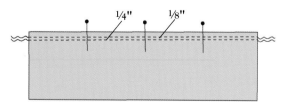

F. Pressing

Pressing is important in sewing and quilting. It really makes your project look professional. You'll also use an iron and ironing board when you're working with fusible web and iron-on interfacing. Make sure that your tools are easily accessible. You may be getting up and down often—I have to admit that it is nice to get up every once in a while!

G. Hemming

I use a few different methods of hemming aprons in this book. They are:

Rolled Hem: One of the easiest ways to make a small rolled hem is by using a hemming foot. This works best on straight edges. I found that clipping a slight angle at the beginning of the fabric helps to get started much quicker. Refer to your sewing machine guide and use a scrap piece of fabric to practice. You'll learn to love this tool, too.

Pressed Rolled Hem:

1. Press fabric ¼" toward the wrong side.

¼"

2. Fold fabric over another ¼" and stitch close to the fold to achieve a clean ¼" hem. Press.

¼"

Rickrack Hem:

1. Spray sizing along the raw edge of the project and press.

2. Sew ¼" stitching line from the raw edge.

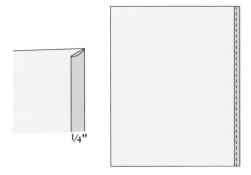

3. Turn along the stitching line toward the wrong side and press. Stitch to hold.

4. Position rickrack, on the right side, with the inside V along the outside edge of the project. (Part of the rickrack will be hanging over the edge.)

5. Stitch down the center of the rickrack. *Note: I found that my ¼" quilting foot was perfect to keep my stitches in the center of the rickrack.*

6. Press rickrack to wrong side. Topstitch, on the front side, ⅛" from the edge. Press.

Double-Fold Bias Tape Hem:

One of the easiest ways to hem your apron is to use packaged double-fold bias tape. If you look closely, you can see that one side of the tape is slightly wider than the other side. Be sure to place the project edge into the fold of the bias tape so that the wider side will be on the back side of the project. You may need to stitch two packages of bias tape together to yield the length needed for the project. Be sure to join the ends with the folds matching to make sure that the bias tape works correctly. Refer to Using Double-Fold Bias Tape to hem your project.

You may also make your own double-fold bias tape. Most packaged bias tape is available in solid colors only. Self-made bias tape for the projects in this book can be made with any 100% cotton fabric. Try a stripe or other geometric print for a great edge finish!

Making Double-fold Bias Tape:

1. Cut and join 1" bias strips in the length needed for the pattern. (See Cutting and Joining Bias Strips on page 13.)

2. Thread one end of the bias strip into a ½" bias tape maker (see Notions), following the manufacturer's directions. Pin the end of the bias strip onto end of ironing board.

3. Apply sizing to bias strip. Keep iron about ½" from tape maker and press as you pull the tool along the bias strip. When you reach the opposite end of the ironing board, re-pin and repeat.

4. Fold the bias tape in half lengthwise, carefully aligning the previously folded edges, and press.

5. Square the ends to create double-fold bias tape.

Using Double-fold Bias Tape:

1. Insert the edge of the project into the fold of the bias tape.

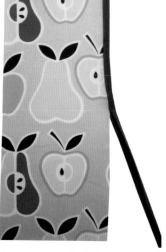

2. Begin stitching at the end of the tape on the inside folded edge.

3. Stitch along the edge 2"–3". Check to be sure that the edge of the bias tape on the back side of the project was caught in the stitching. If it was not, adjust your stitching to place it more onto the bias tape. Stitch, and recheck.

4 Sew the tape around the edge of the project, being sure to keep the edge flat and fully inserted into the fold of the tape. Do not stretch the edge of the project or the bias tape.

5. When approaching the beginning of the tape, stop stitching. Mark the end of the bias tape to overlap the beginning ½" and cut off excess.

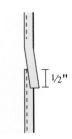

½"

6. Unfold the tape, turn the end under ¼" and refold. Place the folded end over the beginning end to enclose the raw beginning end. Complete sewing.

H. Cutting & Joining Bias Strips

1. Unfold fabric and press flat.

2. Locate the true bias of your fabric by folding it so that the selvage edge is parallel to the crosswise edge.

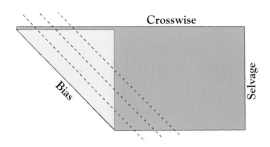

Crosswise

Bias

Selvage

3. Press fabric along the diagonal fold. Position a cutting ruler along the creased fold. Trim ⅛" off the folded edge with a rotary cutter. Cut bias strips, in the width needed for the binding, along the trimmed edge.

4. Sew strips together to make one continuous bias strip in the length needed for the pattern. Press seams open.

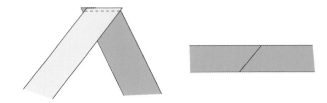

I. Quilting

There are a few projects in this book that will require you to do some quilting. There are two methods that I like to use.

Walking Foot: This is an additional foot that you can purchase for your machine. It helps move the top layer of fabric through your machine at the same pace as the feed dogs. I like to use this method when I want my quilting to be in a straight line. I also use this foot when I attach my bindings to a quilt or quilted item. Be sure when making straight lines that you start sewing from the same edge for each line. If you alternate starting from different edges of the quilt, you may end up with twisted fabric.

Free Motion Quilting: This method uses a darning foot with the feed dogs lowered on your sewing machine. The stitches meander across the project. I really like this method. It may take some practice to get your stitches to look how you want, so make up a "mock" quilt and practice.

1. I use LickityGrip (see Notions) for this method. Apply on your fingertips and rub together. Let dry.

2. If you have a bobbin case, you may need to insert your thread into the little hole to give it more tension and keep it from showing on the top of your quilt.

3. Keep your hands on your quilt on either side of the needle area while moving the quilt under the needle.

4. Use the same color thread in the bobbin and needle of the machine. This helps your stitches look cleaner. If you need to use different colors, adjust your thread tension and stitch on a practice piece to make sure you don't see the bottom thread on the quilt top.

5. The designs for meandering are endless. I used a loopy design for the projects in this book.

6. Most importantly, practice, practice, practice! It is the only way that you will learn to move your quilt under the needle at a speed that produces nice, even stitches.

J. Binding

Preparing Binding

1. If the pattern instructions indicate bias binding, cut bias strips and join them referring to Cutting and Joining Bias Strips on page 13.

2. If straight-grain strips were cut with pattern, join the strips on the short ends with a diagonal seam. Trim seam allowance to ¼". Press the seam open.

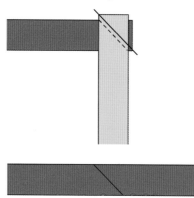

3. Press the strip in half along the length with wrong sides together to complete the binding.

Sewing Binding to the Project

1. Pin prepared binding strip, raw edges together, onto the right side of the project. Sew the binding along the edge, using a 1/4" seam allowance. Stop stitching 1/4" from the corner of project. Backstitch three or four stitches. Cut threads.

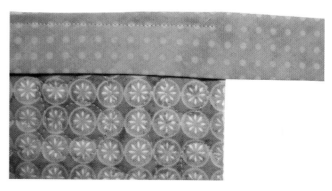

2. Fold binding straight up to be parallel to next edge.

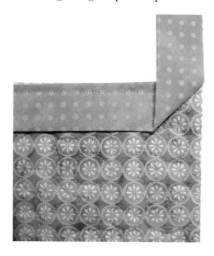

3. Fold binding straight down, so that folded edge is even with raw edge.

4. Start stitching at the edge, backstitching three or four stitches. Continue sewing binding to next corner and repeat steps for each remaining corner.

5. To finish binding, overlap the two end pieces to measure the cut width of the binding strip (usually 2¼" or 2½") and cut straight across.

6. Unfold binding strip. Pin ends right sides together at a 90° angle and sew a diagonal seam. (See Preparing Binding, step 2 on page 14.) Trim the corner, leaving a ¼" seam allowance. Press seam open. Fold strip in half and pin to edge of the project. Complete stitching.

7. Turn binding to back of project and pin so that the fold is covering the stitching line.

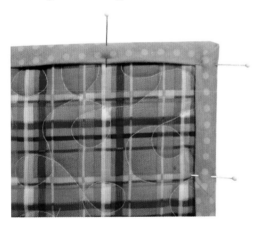

8. With thread to match the top of the project in the needle and thread to match the binding in the bobbin, use the Stitch-in-the-Ditch method along the edge of the binding on the top of the project, being sure to catch the binding edge on the back of the project.

K. Stitch-in-the-Ditch

1. Position your sewing machine needle so that the stitching falls just a fraction of an inch away from the actual seam.

2. Stitch along the seam so your stitches are in the indentation (ditch) made by the seam.

L. Embroidery

I have found several vintage patterns for hand or machine embroidery. Evie's Apron on page 50 uses a machine-embroidery pattern from a CD of vintage-style designs. If you prefer to use a hand-embroidered design, you may want to use a vintage pattern that you have, or try pattern #239 Grandma's Tea Towels by Crab-apple Hill, www.crabapplehillstudio.com. This pattern will give you the same look and feel as the machine-embroidered pattern that I used. For true vintage patterns, check out Aunt Martha's patterns at www.colonialpatterns.com.

HALF APRONS

Chapter 2

Minnie's Apron

This is one of the easiest aprons in the book! Coordinate two beautiful prints to make a reversible apron for yourself or a friend. The addition of satin or grosgrain ribbon and rickrack makes this a winner. This project is great for children and those learning to sew.

Finished Size

17½" square

You will need

* 2 coordinating fat quarters (18" x 22")
* ⅛ yard iron-on woven interfacing
* 2 yards coordinating 1¼"-wide rickrack
* 1½ yards 1½"-wide ribbon
* All-purpose thread to match fabrics and ribbon
* ¼ yard ¼"-wide fusible web
* Chalk pencil
* Anti-fray solution
* Heavy cardboard or template plastic
* Basic sewing supplies, rotary cutting tools, and ¼" quilting foot

Cutting Instructions

1. Cut (1) 18" square from each coordinating fat quarter (apron)
2. Cut (1) 2" x 18" strip from the iron-on interfacing (waistband)

Preparation

1. Place the two apron squares right sides together. Fold the two layers in half vertically. *Note: Line up the side edges perfectly.*
2. Prepare a cardboard or plastic pattern for the 9" circle given on the pullout pattern sheet.

3. Position the circle pattern on the lower right corner (there will be four layers). Mark the curve on the corner with the chalk pencil.
4. Cut around the marked curve to make the rounded bottom corners of the apron.

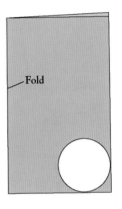

Sewing Instructions

Note: *Please read all instructions before beginning this project. All seams are ¼" wide.*

1. Apply the waistband interfacing strip along the top edge of the wrong side of one of the apron pieces.

2. On the right side of the interfaced piece, sew rickrack along both side edges and the bottom edge, starting at the top right corner and ending at the top left corner. **Note:** *Position the inside curve of the rickrack along the raw edge and sew down the center of the rickrack.*

3. Sew a piece of rickrack across the top straight edge of the interfaced piece.

4. Place the apron pieces right sides together. Sew around the edges, beginning and ending on the top edge and leaving an 8" opening on the top edge. Clip corners. (See Seam Allowance, Grading and Clipping on page 10.)

5. Turn right side out. Fold opening edges to the inside. Press outer edges.

6. Place an 8" length of ¼"-wide fusible web inside the opening on the folded seam allowance and press to secure. Remove paper backing. Press opening closed.

7. Topstitch close to edge around the outside of the apron.

Add the Buttonholes

1. Fold the apron in half vertically. Press to crease the center. Mark 1" on each side of the crease with a pin.

2. Position three more pins, 2" apart, on each side of the center pins. Place a fourth pin on each end 1½" from the third pin.

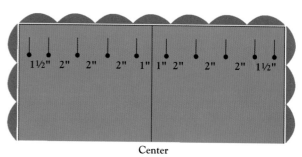

Center

3. With matching thread in needle and bobbin, make a 1⅝"-long buttonhole at each pin, beginning buttonholes ⅜" from top edge of apron. Cut open buttonholes.

4. Thread ribbon through buttonholes making sure ends are the same length. Secure ribbon at each side by stitching to the apron, using thread to match the ribbon.

5. Make notched ends by folding ribbon in half lengthwise and cutting at an angle. Secure ends with anti-fray solution.

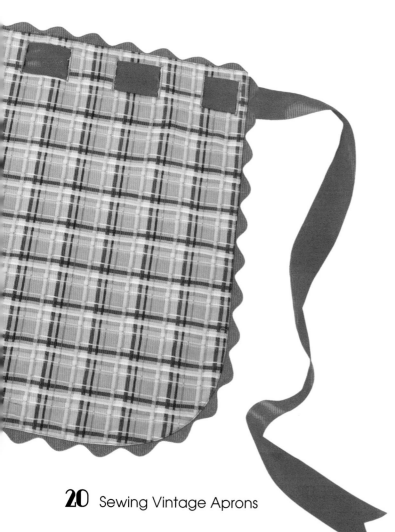

Reversed Side of Apron

This apron is named after my maternal grandmother, who was an excellent cook. I remember her wearing this apron whenever we visited, and she was always at her stove making up some of our favorite No-Bake Cocoa Peanut Drops!

Finished Size
22" x 23"

You will need
* 1⅜ yards floral fabric
* 1 kitchen tea towel to match fabric
* ⅛ yard iron-on woven interfacing
* ¾ yard or 1 package coordinating ½"-wide rickrack
* 1½ yards or 1 package coordinating ¼"-wide rickrack
* ¾ yard ¼"-wide fusible web
* Thread to match fabric, towel, and rickrack
* Anti-fray solution
* Basic sewing supplies, rotary cutting tools, and ¼" quilting foot

Cutting Instructions
1. Cut the following from the floral:
(1) 24" x 42" rectangle (skirt)
(2) 4" x 36" strips (ties)
(1) 4¼" x 23" strip (waistband)
(1) 6¼" square (pocket)
2. From the kitchen tea towel, cut (1) 14" x width of towel piece for the towel and (1) 3¾" x 6¼" rectangle for the pocket trim. **Note:** *Include one hemmed end in the towel piece and the other hemmed end in the pocket trim.*
3. Cut (1) 2¼" x 23" waistband strip from the iron-on interfacing.

Sewing Instructions
Note: *Please read all instructions before beginning this project. All seams are ¼" wide, unless otherwise mentioned.*

1. Make a rolled or pressed rolled hem on each 24" edge of the skirt rectangle. (See Hemming on page 11.)
2. Press ¼" to wrong side on the bottom edge of the skirt. Fold under another 2½" and pin. Topstitch to secure. Press to complete bottom hem.
3. Gather the top raw edge of the skirt to measure 22". (See Gathering on page 10.)

Add the Towel
1. Gather the towel to measure 6" along the cut edge.
2. Pin the gathered towel onto the front right side of skirt 2½" from the side edge. Baste in place.

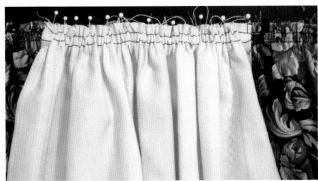

Add the Waistband
1. Press the interfacing strip to one long edge of the wrong side of the 4½" x 23" waistband strip.

2. Press ¼" to the wrong side on the opposite edge of the waistband.

3. Pin the gathered edge of the apron, right sides together, to the interfaced edge of the waistband, leaving ½" on each end of waistband extending beyond the skirt.

4. Sew across the bottom row of gathering stitches, backstitching at each end. Spread gathers evenly while sewing.

5. Trim the gathered seam allowance in half, leaving the waistband seam allowance intact. Press waistband up away from the skirt. (See Seam Allowances, Grading & Clipping on page 10.)

Add the Rickrack

1. Sew ½"-wide rickrack to waistband ⅞" from edge of seam. (The ⅞" will be the actual stitching line along the center of the rickrack.)

2. Sew ¼"-wide rickrack on top of the wider rickrack. Use your seam ripper or stiletto to hold the rickrack in place while you sew.

3. Sew ¼"-wide rickrack 2½" from the hemmed end on the right side of the towel piece. Turn ¼" at each end of the rickrack to the back side of the towel and backstitch at each end. Use anti-fray solution to prevent fraying at ends of rickrack.

Make the Ties

1. Make a rolled or pressed rolled hem on both long edges and one end of each 3½" x 36" tie strip.

2. Fold one hemmed corner at the end of a tie strip to the back to create a 45° angle. Sew across the straight edge. Repeat on the remaining tie strip.

3. Fold waistband in half along the length. Mark the center with a pin at each end.

4. Pin the raw end of a tie strip even with the pin at one end, placing the tie right sides together with the waistband. Make a tuck in the tie strip to fit the waistband. Baste in place. Repeat with the second tie strip on the other end of the waistband.

5. Fold the waistband over to cover the ties, matching the folded edge of the waistband with the seam between the waistband and skirt. Sew across the ends of the waistband with a ½" seam allowance, backstitching at each end of the seams. Cut the seam allowance of the ties in half and clip the corners.

6. Turn the waistband right side out and press the folded edge of the waistband next to waistband/apron seam.

7. Insert a strip of ¼"-wide fusible web inside the waistband on the seam allowance and press to secure. Remove paper backing. Press waistband closed.

8. Topstitch waistband ⅛" from edges on all sides.

Make the Pocket

1. Sew ¼"-wide rickrack on the right side of the towel strip 1" from one 6¼" edge.

2. Place the 6¼" pocket square right side down on your work surface. Place the towel strip right side down on the pocket square with the top and side edges aligned. Pin. **Note:** *The rickrack edge is the top edge of the towel strip.*

3. Sew across the top edge. Zigzag stitch the seam allowance. Press the towel strip up away from the pocket square.

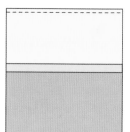

4. Fold the towel strip down over the right side of the pocket square. Stitch along the sides ⅛" from the edges to hold in place. Sew across the bottom of the towel strip. Zigzag stitch the side and bottom edges of the pocket.

5. Press side and bottom edges of the pocket ¼" toward the wrong side. Press.

6. Position and pin the pocket to the apron 5½" from left side of the skirt and 5½" from waistband seam. Stitch close to the side and bottom edges of the pocket, backstitching at each end.

My Grandma Sadie Bower often made this recipe for us. As I made this apron, I grabbed her wooden spoon, put on her apron, and made a batch of these cookies. Her wooden spoon still has cocoa embedded into it. That is how often she made these cookies!

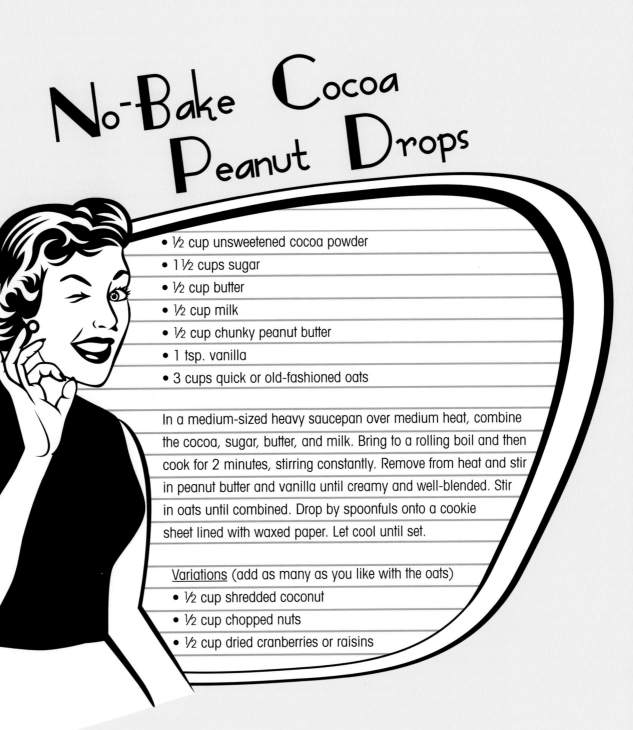

No-Bake Cocoa Peanut Drops

- ½ cup unsweetened cocoa powder
- 1 ½ cups sugar
- ½ cup butter
- ½ cup milk
- ½ cup chunky peanut butter
- 1 tsp. vanilla
- 3 cups quick or old-fashioned oats

In a medium-sized heavy saucepan over medium heat, combine the cocoa, sugar, butter, and milk. Bring to a rolling boil and then cook for 2 minutes, stirring constantly. Remove from heat and stir in peanut butter and vanilla until creamy and well-blended. Stir in oats until combined. Drop by spoonfuls onto a cookie sheet lined with waxed paper. Let cool until set.

Variations (add as many as you like with the oats)
- ½ cup shredded coconut
- ½ cup chopped nuts
- ½ cup dried cranberries or raisins

AILENE'S APRON

I named this apron after my mother. She made this apron and, I believe, was afraid to use it after she put so much handwork into it. It has never been washed. I did not remake this apron because my mother's work is so beautiful!

Finished Size
22" x 23"

You will need

* 1⅜ yards ¼"-square gingham fabric
* ⅛ yard iron-on woven interfacing
* 4 yards or 2 packages contrasting ½"-wide rickrack
* 5½ yards or 2 packages contrasting ¼"-wide rickrack
* ¾ yard ½"-wide fusible web
* Thread to match fabric and rickrack
* 2 skeins coordinating embroidery floss
* Embroidery needle
* Anti-fray solution
* Basic sewing supplies, rotary cutting tools, and ¼" quilting foot

Instructions

Note: Please read all instructions before beginning this project. All seams are ¼".

1. Cut all apron pieces from the gingham and cut the iron-on woven interfacing waistband strip referring to cutting for Sadie's Apron on page 22.

Add the Rickrack
Note: You may choose to add the rickrack with your sewing machine, but I think the hand embroidery is truly vintage!

1. Sew ¼"-wide rickrack 6" from one 42" edge of the apron rectangle, using 2 strands of embroidery floss and a running stitch. Alternate the stitches between the top and bottom of the rickrack. Align the rickrack with a gingham row to make a straight line.

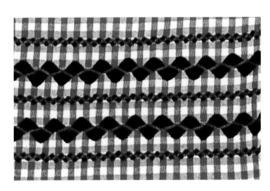

2. Repeat step 1 with a length of ½"-wide rickrack, approximately two rows of gingham (or ½") above the ¼"-wide rickrack. Continue this method to add 2 more rows of 1/4"-wide rickrack and one more row of ½"-wide rickrack.

3. Fold one edge of the pocket square ¼" to the wrong side. Fold under ½" again. Press. Topstitch along fold to hem. Repeat steps 1 and 2 on the pocket, positioning the first row of ¼"-wide rickrack to cover the hem stitching line.

4. Fold the waistband strip in half along the length and press to crease. Unfold the strip. Place the first strip of ¼"-wide rickrack on the first complete row of gingham below the crease (approximately ⅛"–¼" below the crease). Stitch in place as for the apron bottom and pocket. Add two rows of ½"-wide rickrack and one more row of ¼"-wide rickrack referring to the photo below. The last row of ½"-wide rickrack should end ¾" from the raw edge of the waistband.

5. Apply anti-fray solution to each end of the rickrack lengths.

Make the Apron

1. Follow the instructions for Sadie's Apron to hem and gather the skirt and add the waistband and ties. *Note: The interfacing strip on the waistband should cover the back side of the embroidery stitches.*

2. Fold the side and bottom edges of the pocket piece ¼" to the wrong side. Press.

3. Position and pin the pocket to the apron 5½" from left side of the skirt and 5½" from waistband seam. Stitch close to the side and bottom edges of the pocket, backstitching at each end.

My Apron Memory

We live half a block away from my grandparents when I was little. My older brother (by four years) and I were at their house all the time. My grandmother was always cooking, it seemed. There was only one highchair in the kitchen—that was where I was. One day my brother was in a particularly rambunctious mood and getting underfoot. I'm sure my grandmother's intention was to keep him safe, as well as not trip over him while she multitasked prepping the next meal. So what's a grandmother to do? Why grab a spare apron and tie him to a chair with it and move him to the table with something to keep him busy! We were all safe and secure while Sunday dinner was in the works.

Stephanie Girard
West Hartford, Connecticut

ANNIE'S APRON

This is the perfect apron for cooking, cleaning, sewing, and gardening. I've included my family's favorite Buttermilk Biscuits recipe. Write it on a recipe card and place it in the pocket of the apron with a pastry cutter or wooden spoon to make a great gift! And be sure to check out the matching placemats and oven mitts on pages 74 and 76.

Finished Size
21" x 14¾"

You will need
* ½ yard gingham fabric
* ⅓ yard large floral fabric
* ½ yard print fabric
* ⅛ yard iron-on woven interfacing
* All-purpose thread to match fabrics
* ¾ yard ¼"-wide fusible web
* Chalk pencil
* 12" ruler
* Basic sewing supplies, rotary cutting tools, and ¼" quilting foot

Cutting Instructions
1. Cut (1) 13½" x 37" skirt rectangle from the gingham.

2. Cut (1) 7" x 37" pocket rectangle from the large floral.

3. Cut (1) 5" x 25" waistband strip and (2) 4" x 37" tie strips from the print.

4. Cut (1) 2¾" x 25" waistband strip from the iron-on interfacing.

Sewing Instructions
Note: *Please read all instructions before beginning project. All seams are ¼", unless otherwise mentioned.*

Make and Add the Pocket
1. Press ¼" toward wrong side along one 37" edge of the pocket rectangle. Fold under ¾" again and press. Topstitch along both folded edges to hem.

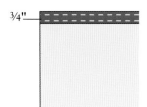

2. Place the skirt piece right side down. Position the hemmed pocket piece right side down on the skirt piece, matching long raw edges. Sew a ¼" seam along the long edge. Press seam open.

3. Fold pocket onto front side of skirt at seam. Press seam flat. Pin edges and baste along the sides.

4. Make a pressed rolled hem on both side edges of the skirt/pocket piece. (See Hemming on page 11.)

5. Fold the skirt/pocket piece in half vertically and mark the center of the pocket with a pin. Mark 6" on either side of center two times to create 6 divisions. With a ruler and chalk pencil, draw a vertical line at each pin. Stitch along lines, backstitching at beginning and end to make six separate pockets.

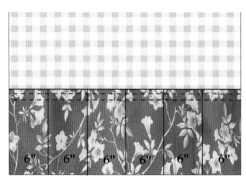

6. Gather the top edge of the skirt to measure 21". Mark the center with a pin. (See Gathering on page 10.)

Add the Waistband

1. Press one long edge of the waistband strip ½" to the wrong side.

2. Press the iron-on interfacing strip onto the wrong side of the opposite edge of the waistband.

3. Place a pin at the center and 2" from each end of waistband.

4. Place the gathered skirt edge, right sides together, with the waistband, matching the center pins. Continue pinning the skirt to the waistband, leaving 2" open at each end of the waistband.

5. Sew skirt to the waistband with a ½" seam allowance, adjusting gathers as you go. Backstitch at beginning and end. Trim the gathered skirt seam allowance in half. (See Seam Allowance, Grading & Clipping on page 10.)

6. Press the waistband up away from the skirt.

Make the Ties

1. Make a rolled or pressed rolled hem on both long sides and one end of each tie strip. (See Hemming on page 11.)

2. Fold the waistband in half along the length to find the center. Mark with a pin.

3. Gather the tie ends to fit half of the width of the waistband. (See Gathering on page 10.)

4. Pin a gathered tie end, right sides together, at each end of the waistband between the bottom seam and the marked center of the waistband. Baste to secure.

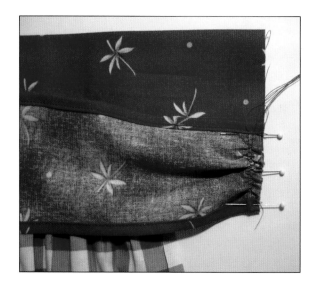

5. Fold the top half of the waistband over to cover the tie. Repeat on other end.

6. Sew ends closed to secure tie inside of waistband. Trim waistband seam in half and trim corner off. Turn right side out.

7. Tuck a strip of ¼" fusible web on the seam allowance inside the waistband opening, press to secure. Remove paper backing. Press waistband closed. Topstitch waistband close to edges on all sides.

Turn to pages 74 and 76 for the matching mitts and placemats.

I have been making this recipe for over 30 years. I got it out of a cooking magazine and altered it just a little. I've given it to friends and family, and they all agree that it is THE BEST biscuit recipe they've ever had. It is now one that will be passed on from generation to generation!

Buttermilk Biscuits

- 2½ cups flour
- 1½ tbsp. sugar
- ½ tsp. cream of tartar
- 1 tsp. baking soda
- ½ tsp. salt
- ½ cup butter, softened
- ⅔ cup buttermilk
- 1 egg

SUGAR

FLOUR

Preheat oven to 425°. Grease a baking sheet. Mix the dry ingredients together. Cut the butter into the dry mix until it resembles a coarse meal. Stir in the buttermilk and egg with a fork. Knead the dough 4 or 5 times in the bowl. Do not handle very much. Dump out onto the prepared baking sheet. Pat into a circle ½" thick. Cut into 8 wedge-shaped pieces (like a pizza). Bake for 15 minutes or until golden brown.

PEARL'S APRON

This pattern came from a very old apron that I found at a secondhand store. It was well used and loved! The ties were practically shredded into strips, and the apron was worn thin. It had to be a favorite for its original owner, and it is for me, too. Enjoy my version of this apron with ribbon on the waistband and in the eyelet trim!

Finished Size
17" x 20"

You will need
* 1¾ yards floral fabric
* 1 yard 1¼"-wide eyelet with opening for ⅜" ribbon
* 1 yard ⅜"-wide ribbon for eyelet
* ⅔ yard 1"-wide ribbon for waistband
* ⅛ yard iron-on woven interfacing
* Thread to match fabric and ribbons
* 1¾ yards ¼"-wide fusible web
* Basic sewing supplies, rotary cutting tools, and ¼" quilting foot

Cutting Instructions

1. Prepare tissue paper patterns for the Pearl's Apron pieces given on the pullout pattern sheet. (See Transferring Patterns on page 10.)

2. Unfold the floral fabric and press flat. Fold the floral fabric in half across the width, matching the raw ends, to make a 31½" x 42" piece. Place the Lower Skirt pattern on the fold of the fabric and cut out.

Lower Skirt
42"
31½"

3. Unfold the remainder of the fabric. Measure and mark 20" on the adjacent sides of one corner of the fabric. Fold the corner over on the marks. Place the Upper Skirt pattern on the fold and cut out.

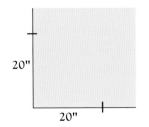

20"
20"
Upper Skirt

4. Cut (2) 4½" x 36" tie strips and (1) 5" x 17½" waistband strip from the remainder of the fabric.
Note: *I made a set of matching Circle Oven Mitts (see page 78). Cut (4) 10" squares from the remaining fabric to make a set, if desired.*

5. Cut a 45° angle on one end of each tie piece.

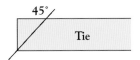

45°
Tie

6. Cut (1) 2½" x 17½" waistband strip from the iron-on woven interfacing.

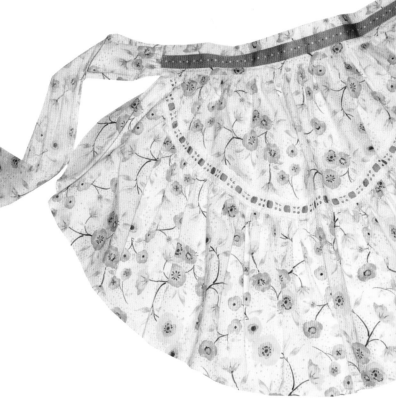

Sewing Instructions

Note: Please read all instructions before beginning project. All seams are ¼", unless otherwise mentioned.

Make the Upper Skirt

1. Make a rolled or pressed rolled hem along the curved bottom edge of the upper skirt piece, turning the hem to the right side, not the wrong side. This will give you a finished edge on the back side. (See Hemming on page 11.)

2. Press a strip of ¼" fusible web along the edge of the hem. Do not remove paper backing.

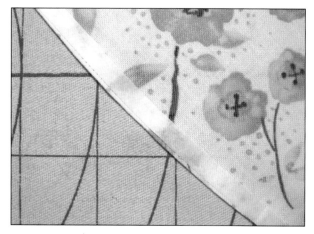

3. Pin upper skirt to ironing board with right side up.

4. Pin eyelet around hem, at lower edge, so that one edge of the eyelet is just covering the fusible web.

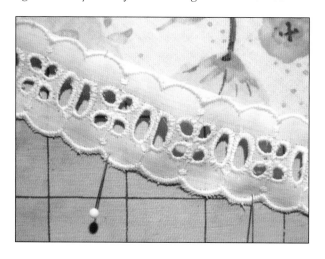

5. Gently iron eyelet so that it eases along upper skirt hem. Try not to make creases in eyelet. Keep the eyelet and skirt pinned to the ironing board.

6. Remove the paper backing from the fusible web and press eyelet to upper skirt.

7. Remove upper skirt from ironing board and trim ends of eyelet.

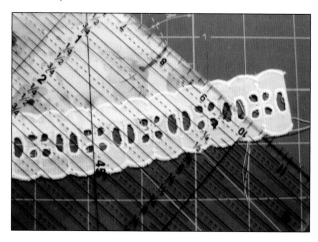

8. Sew along the edge of the eyelet to secure to the upper skirt.

Make the Lower Apron

1. Make a pressed rolled hem on the bottom and side edges of the lower skirt. (See Hemming on page 11.)

2. Press the top edge ⅛" toward right side of fabric. *Note: This will give you a clean edge on the back of apron. The raw edges will be covered on the front with eyelet trim.*

3. Gather the top edge to measure 32". (See Gathering on page 10.)

4. Fold the lower skirt piece in half vertically and mark the center of the gathered edge with a pin. Repeat with the upper skirt piece and mark the center of the bottom eyelet edge with a pin.

5. Pin the lower skirt center under the upper skirt center, matching pins, and secure with a pin. **Note:** *The right side of the gathered lower skirt will be against the wrong side of the upper skirt, just under the eyelet.*

6. Pin each end of the lower skirt to the ends of the upper skirt, leaving ¼" of the upper skirt extending on each end to insert into waistband seam. Adjust gathers and pin where needed.

7. Sew across edge of lace and then sew another row close to gathers. Trim all threads. Press.

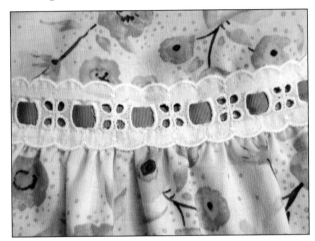

8. Thread the ⅜" ribbon through the eyelet and stitch across each end to secure.

Add the Waistband

1. Press the interfacing strip along one long edge on the wrong side of the waistband strip. Turn the remaining long edge of the waistband strip ¼" to the wrong side. Press.

2. Gather the top edge of the upper skirt to measure 17".

3. Find the center of the upper skirt and the interfaced edge of the waistband and mark with pins.

4. Pin the skirt, right sides together, with the waistband, leaving ¼" extending on both ends of the waistband. Even up gathers as you go.

5. Sew the skirt to the waistband. Trim the gathered seam allowance in half. Press the waistband up and away from the skirt. (See Seam Allowance, Grading & Clipping on page 10.)

6. Pin the 1" ribbon along the waistband ½" from the waistband/apron seam. Stitch along both edges of the ribbon, using thread to match the ribbon.

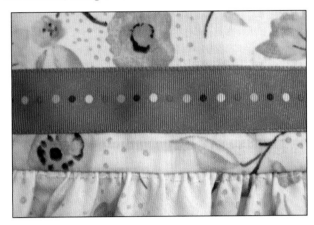

Make the Ties

1. Make a rolled hem or pressed rolled hem along the long sides of each tie strip and across the 45° angled end.

2. Complete the apron referring to steps 2–7 of Make the Ties for Annie's Apron on page 32. **Note:** *When pinning the tie ends to the waistband, position the ties so that the longest side edge of the tie is at the bottom edge of the waistband.*

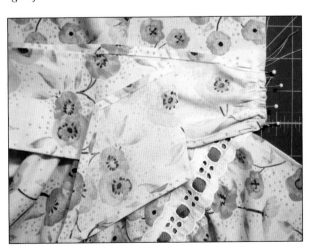

EVELYN'S APRON

I named this apron after my Grandma Evelyn Tanner. She always wore an apron with pockets. This apron was made years ago to hold clothespins or vegetables or fruit from her garden, thus the large one-piece pocket! One of her favorite desserts was peach cobbler with a white sauce.

Finished size
21" x 18"

You will need
* ⅔ yard large floral fabric
* ⅛ yard small floral fabric
* ⅛ yard iron-on woven interfacing
* 4 yards or 2 packages coordinating ½"-wide rickrack
* Thread to match each fabric
* ¾ yard ¼"-wide fusible web
* Spray sizing
* Basic sewing supplies, rotary cutting tools, and ¼" quilting foot

Cutting Instructions
1. Prepare tissue paper patterns for the Evelyn's Apron pieces given on the pullout pattern sheet. (See Transferring Patterns on page 10.)

2. Cut the Skirt piece on the fold of the large floral and the Pocket piece on the fold of the small floral.

3. From the remainder of the small floral, cut (2) 4½" x 42" tie strips and (1) 4½" x 21" waistband strip.

4 Cut (1) 2½" x 21" waistband strip from the iron-on woven interfacing.

Sewing Instructions
Note: Please read all instructions before beginning project. All seams are ¼".

Add the Pocket
1. Sew rickrack around the side and bottom edges of the pocket piece. (See Rickrack Hem on page 11.)

2.. Fold the skirt piece in half vertically and mark the center of the top edge with a pin. Repeat with the pocket piece. Place the pocket right side up on the right side of the skirt, matching center pins. Baste across the top edge. Leave one pin to mark the center.

3. Pin the pocket edges to the skirt. Topstitch close to the side and bottom edges of the pocket, beginning and ending 8" from the top edge. Backstitch at beginning and end. There should be an opening on each side of the pocket.

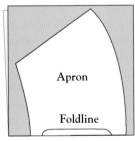
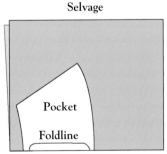
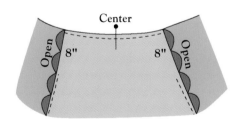

4. Place a pin 3½" on each side of the center pin on the top edge of the skirt. Fold the side pins to the center and pin through all layers to create a pleat. Baste to secure. Press pleat using spray sizing.

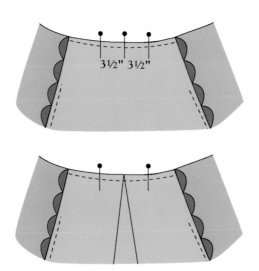

Make the Waistband

1. Press the interfacing strip along one long edge on the wrong side of waistband strip. Turn the remaining long edge of the waistband strip ¼" to the wrong side. Press.

2. Fold the waistband in half across the width and mark the center of the interfaced edge with a pin. Place the waistband, right sides together, with the top edge of the skirt, matching the center pins. Pin in place, leaving 1¼" of the waistband extending at each end.

3. Sew waistband to skirt. **Note:** *Ease skirt waist just a little. If the skirt is pulled too tight, the pleat will not lay flat.* Clip curves in seam allowance.

Make the Ties

1. Make a rolled hem or pressed rolled hem along the long sides of each tie strip. (See Hemming on page 11.)

2. Fold tie ends lengthwise in half, with right sides together, and sew across the folded ends. Turn right side out to create a point. Press.

3. Insert a small piece of ¼" fusible web inside tie point. Press in place. Remove paper backing and press to secure.

4. Complete the apron referring to steps 2–7 in Make the Ties for Annie's Apron on page 32.

My father worked for the U.S. Department of Agriculture and brought home lots of peaches and other fruit. So, we canned, made jam, and baked. I loved and still love making cobblers, and this recipe is the best! Try it with other fruits.

Fresh Peach Cobbler

- 4 cups peaches, peeled and sliced
- 1½ tbsp. cornstarch
- ¼ cup to ⅓ cup brown sugar
- ½ cup water
- 2 tbsp. butter
- ½ tsp. lemon juice

Topping
- ½ cup flour
- ½ cup sugar
- ½ tsp. baking powder
- ¼ tsp. salt
- 2 tbsp. butter, softened
- 1 egg

Preheat oven to 400°. In a saucepan, mix the peaches with the next 3 ingredients. Cook on medium heat until thickened, about 15 minutes. Add the butter and lemon juice. Pour into a greased 8"-round baking dish.

In a medium-sized bowl, beat all topping ingredients with a spoon until smooth. Drop over the top of the cobbler. Bake for 40–50 minutes.

Spiced Honey Cream
- 1 cup heavy cream
- 2 tbsp. honey
- ½ tsp. cinnamon

Beat the heavy cream until thick. Add honey and cinnamon. Drop over the top of the cobbler to serve.

FULL APRONS
Chapter 3

When I saw this print at the store, I knew it had to be an apron! When I showed it to my daughter, Erin, she fell in love with it, and so I named it after her. With a fun and big print like this you should use a simpler pattern to see more of the fabric. Make the pockets as I did or use the coordinating print for a different look.

Finished Length

Approximately 36" from shoulders

You will need

* ✻ 1½ yards main print fabric
* ✻ ½ yard coordinating print fabric
* ✻ 6 yards self-made or 2 packages ¼"-wide double-fold bias tape to contrast with main fabric
* ✻ Scrap of iron-on woven interfacing
* ✻ Thread to match fabrics and bias tape
* ✻ 2 (1¼"-diameter) round buttons
* ✻ Temporary spray adhesive
* ✻ Chalk pencil
* ✻ Basic sewing supplies, rotary cutting tools, and ¼" quilting foot

Cutting Instructions

1. Prepare tissue paper patterns for the Erin's Apron pieces given on the pullout pattern sheet. Transfer all marks on the patterns to the fabric pieces, using the chalk pencil. (See Transferring Patterns on page 10.)

2. Cut the Apron piece on the lengthwise fold of the main print. **Note:** *There are two size ranges marked on the pattern for this apron. Follow the fold and facing lines for your size when cutting the pieces.*

3. Cut (2) Facing pieces and (4) Pocket pieces from the remainder of the main print.

4. Cut (2) 4" x 42" tie strips from the coordinating print.

5. Optional: Cut the Pocket pieces from the coordinating print instead of the main print to give your apron a different look.

Sewing Instructions

Note: *Please read all instructions before beginning this project. All seams are ¼".*

Prepare the Facing

1. With right sides together, sew the facing pieces together along the center front. Press seam open.

2. Turn the bottom edge of the facing under ¼" to the wrong side and stitch across to hem. Press.

3. Iron a scrap of interfacing onto the wrong side of the facing, where buttons and buttonholes will be placed, for stability.

4. Lightly apply temporary spray adhesive to the wrong side of the facing piece.

5. Place the facing piece wrong sides together with the apron. Press to hold the pieces together.

Selvage edges

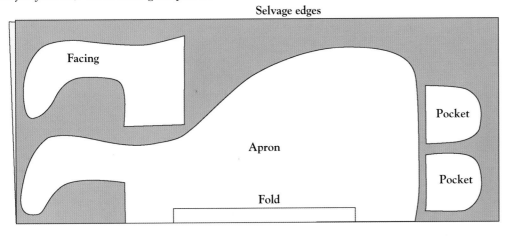

6. Stay stitch around the neckline and shoulder straps. Clip into the neckline corners.

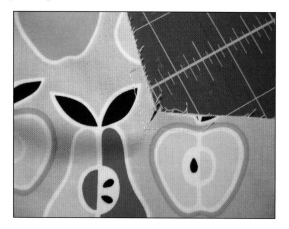

Make the Pockets

1. Place two pocket pieces right sides together. Sew across the top straight edge. Press seam open.

2. Lightly apply temporary spray adhesive to the wrong side of one pocket piece and press the pocket pieces wrong sides together. Topstitch 1" from the top edge.

3. Repeat steps 1 and 2 with the remaining pocket pieces.

4. If using packaged double-fold bias tape, sew the two lengths together on the ends to make a continuous strip, making sure that the folds match from strip to strip. Press seam open. Refold bias tape.

5. Sew bias tape around the pockets, leaving ½" extending beyond the top edges. (See Using Bias Tape on page 12.)

6. Tuck bias ends to the back side of the pockets. Pin the pockets onto the apron piece, referring to the pattern for placement. Sew on top of previous stitching, backstitching at beginning and end.

Hem the Apron

1. Sew bias tape around the edges of the apron, beginning and ending where marked on pattern. (See Using Bias Tape on page 12.)

Make the Ties:

1. Fold ties lengthwise in half with right sides together. Sew along the long side and one short end. Trim off corners. Turn right side out and press. Topstitch close to edge.

2. Pin a tie onto the apron with raw end extending ¼" over the solid end line of the tie placement markings. Stitch on the solid line, backstitching at each end.

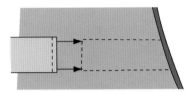

3. Turn the tie over and fold the stitched line to the dashed vertical line of the placement markings, making a tuck in the apron. Sew across the tie, close to the edge of the fold, and along the edges of the tie to the outside edge of the apron. Backstitch at each end. Stitch in the ditch of the binding. (See Stitch-in-the-Ditch on page 15.)

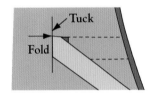
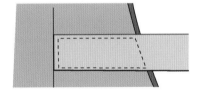

Add Buttonholes and Buttons

1. Make two 1¼" buttonholes at the placement lines on apron neck/shoulder strap. Cut open.

2. Try apron on and pin neck straps together to make the best fit. Use pins to mark placement for your buttons. Sew buttons on.

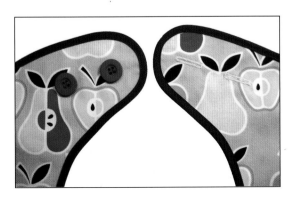

My Apron Memory

I have a few apron memories. One is of my dad wearing mom's old apron (it looked like a short housecoat and buttoned in the front) over his church clothes on Sundays. I also have a more recent memory. A few Christmases ago, I was finally old enough, and married, to be included with all of the ladies of my family. We all received homemade aprons from my aunt. All of them were the same style, in a few different colors. I thought that was so great, and I think of them all when I use it.

My most recent memory is of my two girls, my son and me all wearing aprons to bake cookies. I wish I could sew well enough to make us matching aprons with variations in color, but I love that they all want to wear them when they bake with me.

Annaleesa Hanks
St. Johns, Florida

Evie's Apron

Most people envision vintage aprons with rickrack and embroidery—this apron has both.
The basket of flowers was machine embroidered, but can easily be hand embroidered.
There are lots of vintage and vintage-looking designs available. See page 15 for reference.

Finished Length
Approximately 35" from the shoulder

You will need
* 1½ yards ivory fabric
* 3½ yards or 2 packages coordinating ½"-wide rickrack
* Thread to match fabric and rickrack
* Machine or hand embroidery pattern of choice
* Machine embroidery thread or embroidery floss as required for pattern
* ½ yard tear-away fabric stabilizer for machine embroidery
* 2 (¾") D-rings
* Chalk pencil
* Basic sewing supplies, rotary cutting tools, and ¼" quilting foot

Project Note
This apron has plenty of space to decorate using a multitude of design techniques. I chose to use machine embroidery, but it would be wonderful with hand stitching, appliqué or a painted design. Or if you prefer, use a floral or busy print so there is no need to add decoration at all.

This pattern is also perfect for a man's apron. Square the pocket and apron corners and use a pressed rolled hem around the edges.

Cutting Instructions
1. Prepare tissue paper patterns for the Evie's Apron pieces given on the pullout pattern sheet. Transfer all marks on the patterns to the fabric pieces, using the chalk pencil. (See Transferring Patterns on page 10.)

2. Cut the Apron piece on the lengthwise fold of the ivory fabric. **Note:** *There are two size ranges marked on the pattern for this apron. Follow the fold lines for your size when cutting the pieces.*

3. Cut (2) 3" x 34" tie strips along the selvage edge.

4. Cut (1) Pocket piece from the remainder of the ivory fabric.

5. Cut (1) 2½" x 30" neck strap, (1) 2½" x 6" D-ring strip, and (1) 2¾" x 12¾" facing strip from the remainder of the ivory fabric.

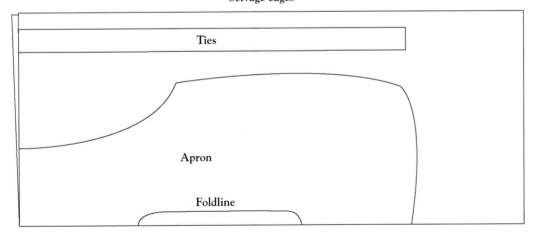

Selvage edges

Ties

Apron

Foldline

Sewing Instructions

Note: Please read all instructions before beginning project. All seams are ¼".

Make the Neck Straps

1. Fold the 6" D-ring strip in half along the 6" side with right sides together. Sew along the long edge. Backstitch at each end. Turn right side out. Press. Topstitch close to all edges.

2. Slide the D-rings onto the D-ring strip. Fold the strip in half to form a loop. Stitch across the strip close to the bottom of the D-rings to secure. Stitch across the raw ends. Backstitch at each end of the seams.

3. Fold the neck strap lengthwise in half with right sides together. Sew across one short end and along the long edge. Trim off corners. Turn right out. Press. Topstitch close to all edges.

Make the Apron

1. Make a pressed rolled hem on the armhole curves. Press. (See Hemming on page 11.)

2. Pin D-ring strap and neck strap to the right side of the apron top with raw edges aligned, leaving ½" on each side. Baste to secure. Pin ends of straps to front of apron to keep out of way for next steps.

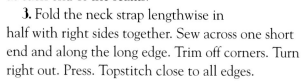

Make the Facing

1. Press one 12¾" facing strip edge ¼" to the wrong side.

2. Pin the raw edge of the facing strip, right sides together, with the top raw edge of the apron, leaving a least ¼" of the facing extending at each end. Trim excess to leave ¼". Stitch in place.

3. Press facing up and topstitch close to seam.

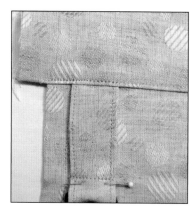

4. Press ¼" at each end of the facing to the wrong side. Press and pin the facing to the wrong side of the apron. Topstitch facing along the sides and across the bottom edge.

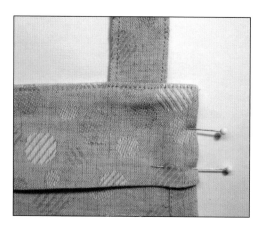

Make the Pocket

1. Make a pressed rolled hem on the top edge of the pocket piece. Press.

2. Make a rickrack hem on the pocket with a ½" rickrack overhang at each end. (See Rickrack Hem on page 11.)

3. Tuck the rickrack ends under the pocket and pin pocket into pocket position marked on the apron. Stitch close to rickrack edge, backstitching at each end.

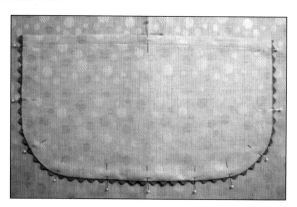

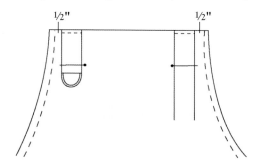

4. Find the center of the pocket and stitch a vertical line from top to bottom to divide the pocket into two sections. Backstitch at each end.

Hem the Apron

1. Make a rickrack hem along the bottom and side edges of the apron. (See Rickrack Hem on page 11.)

Make the Ties:

1. With right sides together, fold each tie lengthwise in half. Sew along long side and one short end. Trim off corners. Turn right side out and press. Topstitch close to edge.

2. Pin the ties 1¼" from the sides of the apron with seam at bottom edge. Stitch across end using a ¼" seam allowance.

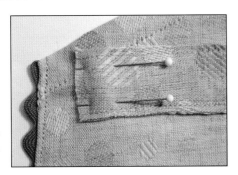

3. Fold the ties over to the outside, enclosing the seam allowances under the ties. Topstitch in place.

4. Embroider the top of the apron as desired, using tear-away fabric stabilizer on the back side of the apron for machine embroidery.

LIZZIE'S APRON

This is another favorite apron of mine. I just love the ruffles and plainness of the apron. There are two options for the straps on this apron. Traditionally the straps crisscrossed in the back and were attached to the waistband near the ties. If you prefer, you may keep the straps loose and tie them around your neck. Have someone help you adjust the positioning of the crisscrossed straps.

Finished Length

Approximately 41½" from the shoulders

You will need

* 1⅞ yards print fabric
* ¼ yard pocket lining fabric
* 10 yards self-made or 3 packages contrasting ¼"-wide double-fold bias tape
* Thread to match print and bias tape
* Temporary spray adhesive
* 2 (⅝"-diameter) buttons
* Chalk pencil
* Hand sewing needle
* Basic sewing supplies, rotary cutting tools, and ¼" quilting foot

Cutting Instructions

1. Prepare tissue paper patterns for the Lizzie's Apron pieces given on the pullout pattern sheet. Transfer all marks on the patterns to the fabric pieces, using the chalk pencil. (See Transferring Patterns on page 10.)

2. Cut the Apron piece on the lengthwise fold of the print fabric. Cut (2) Shoulder Straps along the selvage edge. Cut (2) Ruffle Base pieces, (2) 9" x 8" ruffle pieces and (2) Pocket pieces.

3. From the remainder of the fabric, cut (4) 9" x 8" ruffle pieces (to total 6) and (2) 5" x 30" tie strips.

4. Cut (2) Pocket pieces from the lining fabric.

Sewing Instructions

Note: Please read all instructions before beginning project. All seams are ¼", unless otherwise mentioned.

Make the Ruffles

1. Sew bias tape along one 9" edge of each ruffle piece, chaining the pieces together as you sew. (See Using Double-Fold Bias Tape on page 12.)

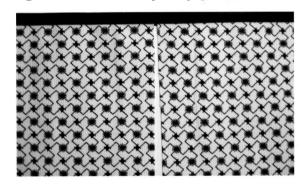

2. Cut ruffle pieces apart.

3. Press ¼" to the wrong side on the 9" raw edge of each ruffle piece.

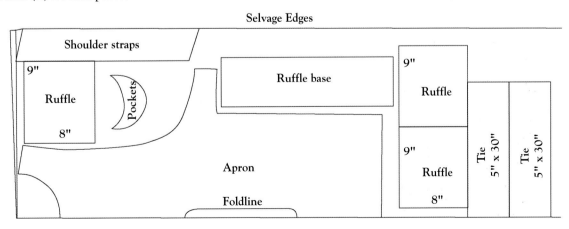

4. Sew 2 rows of gathering stitches across the folded edges. Gather the edges to measure 5½". (See Gathering on page 10.)

5. Pin a ruffle onto each ruffle base ¼" above the ruffle placement 1 line, leaving ¼" of the base piece extending below the ruffle and matching the side edges of the ruffles to the side edges of the ruffle bases. Sew across the gathered edge of the ruffles.

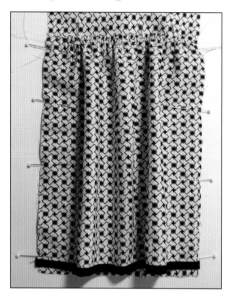

6. Sew along the side edges of the ruffles, using a ⅛" seam allowance.

7. Pin and sew the second ruffles on the ruffle placement 2 chalk lines. Stitch along the side edges. The second ruffles will overlap the bottom ruffles approximately 1¾". Repeat with the top ruffles on the ruffle placement 3 chalk lines.

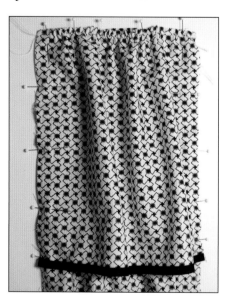

Sew Ruffle Base to Apron

1. Stay stitch the inside corner on the apron piece. Clip to stitched line. (See Stay Stitching on page 10.)

2. Pin and sew the apron piece, right sides together, to the top and side edges of one ruffle base.

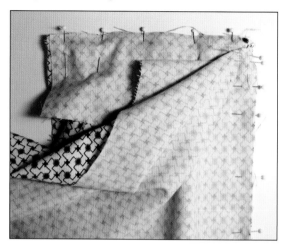

3. Zigzag stitch along the seam allowance to prevent fraying. Press seam toward the apron piece. Repeat with the second ruffle base.

4. Topstitch on the right side of the apron close to the ruffle base seams.

Add the Straps

1. Sew straps to apron front at shoulders. Zigzag stitch seam allowance. Press. ***Note:*** *Be sure to position the diagonal edge of the straps correctly so that they will cross in the back. It is helpful to lay them out with the apron before sewing.*

Add the Bias Tape Hem

1. Stay stitch around apron raw edges to keep from stretching. (See Stay Stitching on page 10.)

2. Sew the bias tape together to make a strip at least 260".

3. Tuck the apron edge inside the bias tape and stitch close to the inside folded edge. I use my ¼" quilting foot so I can see the bias tape and where I am stitching. Begin sewing around the neckline at the end of a neck strap. Stop at corners, cut threads and begin sewing on the next side as if you are beginning over. The bias tape will make its own mitered corners. (See Using Double-Fold Bias Tape on page 12.)

Add the Pockets

1. Apply temporary spray adhesive to the wrong side of the pocket lining pieces. Place a print pocket piece, wrong sides together, with a lining piece. Repeat to make a second pocket.

2. Stitch the bias tape to the top edge of each pocket.

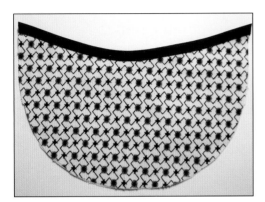

3. Bind the outside edge of pocket, leaving ½" of bias tape extending at the beginning and end. Chain sew with the other pocket, leaving 1" between the pockets. Cut apart, leaving ½" of the binding on each pocket.

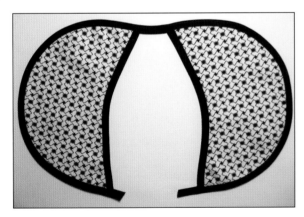

4. With a hand needle, sew a button onto the center top edge of each pocket.

5. Tuck the bias tape ends to the wrong side of the pockets. Pin and sew pockets onto the apron, stitching close to the outside edges. Backstitch at the beginning and end.

Make the Ties

1. Fold a tie strip lengthwise in half with right sides together. Sew along the long edge, stopping 2" from the end. Pivot and stitch to the opposite corner to create a diagonal end. Trim off corner. Turn right side out and press. Topstitch close to edge. Repeat with the second tie strip.

2. Pin ties to the front of the apron approximately 1" from apron edge at waist, positioning ties with the seam side toward the bottom of the apron. Sew along the raw ends and ¼" from the raw ends, backstitching at each end.

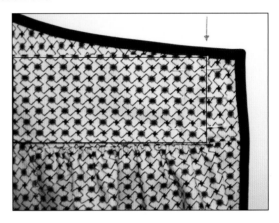

3. Fold the ties over the apron edge, enclosing the raw ends of the tie strips. Stitch along the inside edge of the bias tape, backstitching at the beginning and end.

Sew the Shoulder Strap

1. Pin and sew the right shoulder strap to the back of the left side of the apron. Repeat with the left shoulder strap on the right side of the apron, crossing the straps in the back. You may need some help to find the perfect place for the shoulder straps to make the best fit. Be sure to tie at the waist before pinning the straps in place .

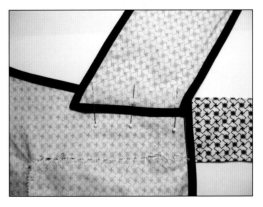

JANE'S APRON

When I saw this fabric with its coordinating print, I knew I wanted to make this apron. It's reversible and uses self-made binding. Don't worry—my instructions make it easy, very easy! I wanted to use vintage buttons on the neck strap and was amazed that I had the perfect color! Search through your button collection to add just the right finishing touch.

Finished Length
Approximately 39" from the shoulder

You will need
* 1⅓ yards print fabric for apron front
* 1¾ yards coordinating fabric for apron back and binding
* ½ yard iron-on woven interfacing
* Thread to match fabrics
* 2 (1") buttons
* ½" bias tape maker
* Temporary spray adhesive
* Chalk pencil
* Basic sewing supplies, rotary cutting tools, and ¼" quilting foot

Cutting Instructions
1. Prepare tissue paper patterns for the Jane's Apron pieces given on the pullout pattern sheet. Transfer all marks on the patterns to the fabric pieces, using the chalk pencil. (See Transferring Patterns on page 10.)

2. Layer the folded print fabric on the folded coordinating print fabric, carefully aligning the folded edges. Pin along the fold to secure.

3. Cut the Apron piece on the lengthwise fold of the fabrics. Cut (2) Pocket pieces and (2) Neck Strap pieces from each fabric.

4. Cut (2) 2½" x 36" tie strips from each fabric.

5. Fold the interfacing in half along the length. Cut (1) facing piece on the fold.

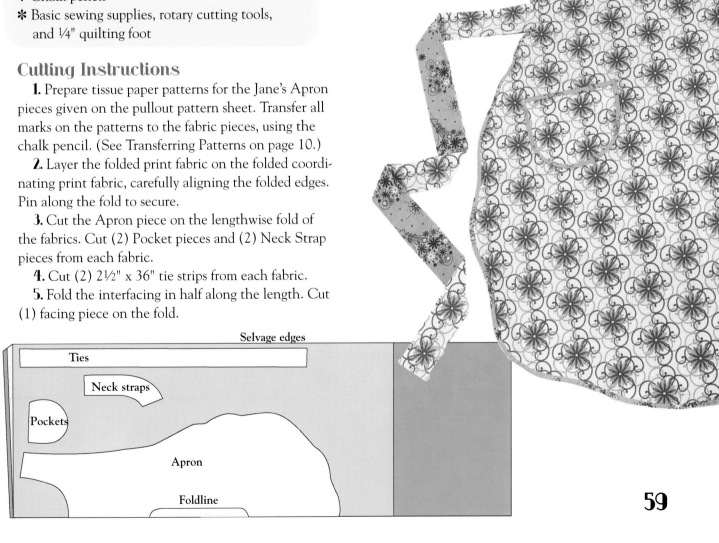

Selvage edges

Ties

Neck straps

Pockets

Apron

Foldline

Sewing Instructions

Note: Please read all instructions prior to making project. All seams are ¼".

1. Iron the interfacing piece onto the wrong side of apron front piece.

2. Sew the neck straps to the shoulders of the apron pieces. Press seams open.

Make the Pockets

1. Make 230" of double-fold bias tape from the coordinating fabric. (See Making Double-Fold Bias Tape on page 12.)

2. Hem the top edge of each pocket using the bias tape. Hem the curved edges of each pocket, leaving a ½" overhang at each end.

3. Tuck the bias tape ends to the back side of the pockets. Pin the pockets in place on the apron front and back pieces.

4. Sew around the curved edges of each pocket on the bias tape stitching line. Backstitch at each end.

Make the Apron

1. Position the aprons on top of each other with right sides out. Apply temporary spray adhesive between the layers to hold together. Pin around the edges.

2. Baste ⅛" from all edges. Do not stretch the fabric around the curves.

3. Sew bias tape around the edges, beginning at the neck straps. Sew the short straight end of the neck straps first, then around the curve of the neck, then the apron. (See Using Double-Fold Bias Tape on page 12.)

4. Make two 1" buttonholes at the placement lines on the neck strap. Cut open.

5. Try the apron on and pin the neck straps together to make the best fit. Use pins to mark placement for your buttons. Sew buttons on.

Make the Ties

1. Place a print fabric tie strip right sides together with a coordinating print tie strip. Stitch along the long edges and across one end. Repeat with the remaining tie strips.

2. Clip corners, turn right side out and press.

3. Place a tie strip with the front fabric side together with the apron front approximately ½" from one side edge. Pin to hold. Sew the end to the apron, backstitching at each end.

4. Flip tie over and topstitch to the bound edge of the apron, backstitching at each end. Repeat with the remaining tie strip on the opposite side.

GRACE'S APRON

I love how this apron turned out! The pocket and bodice piping with rickrack really adds a special touch to the look of this apron. I almost didn't make this apron until a friend fell in love with the big pockets! So, here's to you Mary Alice!

Finished Length

Approximately 30" from the shoulders

You will need

* ⁂ 1⅔ yards floral fabric
* ⁂ ½ yard dark coordinating fabric for piping trim
* ⁂ ½ yard facing fabric
* ⁂ ½ yard iron-on woven interfacing
* ⁂ Thread to match fabrics and rickrack
* ⁂ 3 yards ⅛" piping cord or 1 package maxi piping
* ⁂ 5½ yards or 2 packages ½" rickrack
* ⁂ 1 yard ¼"-wide fusible web
* ⁂ 2 (1¼"-diameter) buttons
* ⁂ Chalk pencil
* ⁂ Basic sewing supplies, rotary cutting tools, ¼" quilting foot, and zipper foot or tricot foot

Cutting Instructions

1. Prepare tissue paper patterns for the Grace's Apron pieces given on the pullout pattern sheet, including the facing pattern and interfacing pattern. Transfer all marks on the patterns to the fabric pieces, using the chalk pencil. (See Transferring Patterns on page 10.)

2. Cut (2) 3½" x 36" tie strips from the floral.

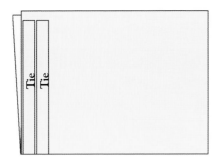

3. Unfold fabric. Fold one selvage edge over 7¼". Cut Apron Front piece on the lengthwise fold.

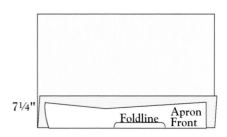

4. Fold one end of fabric over 21". Cut (2) Side Skirt pieces. Trim or fold the bottom edge of the pattern on the curve line. Cut (2) Back Skirt pieces.

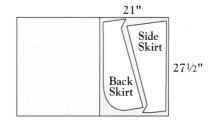

5. Fold the remaining fabric in half. Cut (2) Neck Strap pieces and (2) Pocket pieces.

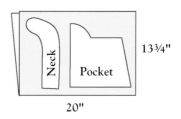

6. Cut the Apron Front Facing piece on the fold of the facing fabric. Cut (2) Neck Strap facing pieces and (2) Pocket facing pieces.

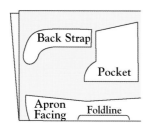

7. Fold the iron-on woven interfacing in half lengthwise. Cut the Apron Front interfacing piece on the fold. Cut (4) 1½" x 6" skirt interfacing strips.

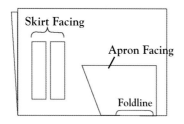

Sewing Instructions

Note: *Please read all instructions before beginning project. All seams are ¼".*

Make the Piping

1. Cut and join 1" bias strips to yield an 80" length. (See Cutting & Joining Bias Strips on page 13.)

2. Fold the bias strip around the piping cord or maxi piping. Align the long raw edges of the bias strip. Stitch close to piping edge with the zipper or tricot foot. You'll need to move your needle as close to the piping as possible.

Make the Apron Front

1. Press the apron front interfacing piece onto the wrong side of the apron front top edge.

2. Place the piping along the edge of the right side of the apron front with raw edges aligned, beginning at the waistline marking. With a zipper or tricot foot, sew piping along the edge ending at the waistline marking. **Note:** *Fold piping at a right angle at beginning and end for ease of construction later on. Put your needle in the down position when turning corners. Clip piping at corners just to the piping stitching line.*

3. Sew rickrack on top of the piping with the zipper or tricot foot, placing one edge of the rickrack slightly over the piping stitching line.

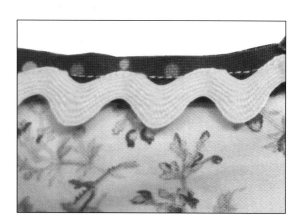

4. Turn apron facing bottom edge ¼" to the wrong side. Stitch along edge. Press.

5. Sew facing, right sides together, to apron front, leaving 3" unstitched at the bottom of each side edge. Clip curves and corners. Turn right side out and press.

Make the Pockets

1. Sew piping onto right side of pocket top edge in the same manner as the apron front, clipping into the inside corner. Repeat with the second pocket.

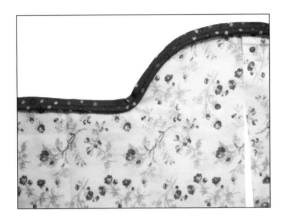

2. Sew rickrack over piping as in step 3 of Make the Apron Front.

3. Pin and sew a pocket facing piece, right sides together, across the top and bottom edges of the pocket, leaving both sides open. Clip curves and corner. Turn right side out and press. Repeat with the second pocket.

4. Pin the pockets onto the side skirt pieces, 5½" from the top edges of the skirt pieces. **Note:** *The straight side edges of the pockets match to the straight edges of the side skirt pieces. Trim edges even, if necessary.*

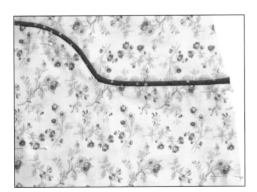

5. Sew along the side and bottom edges of the pockets, leaving the top edge open.

Add the Apron Sides and Back

1. Press a skirt interfacing strip to the top edge of each skirt side and back piece, aligning the top of the strip with the Fold line marked on the fabric pieces.

2. Press the top edge of the skirt pieces ¼" to the wrong side. Stitch across edge.

3. Place the right skirt side and back pieces, right sides together, matching the curved edges and extended top edges. Sew along the length. Clip at the fold line. Press the seam open. Zigzag stitch the edges of the seam allowance. Repeat with the left skirt pieces.

4. Press the top edge of each skirt piece to the wrong side to cover the interfacing strips. Tuck a piece of ¼"-wide fusible web under the folded edge. Press. Remove paper backing. Press folded edge to back of apron to hold in place.

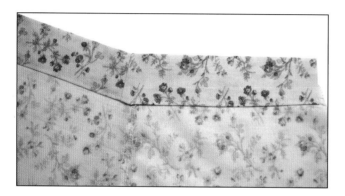

5. Pin and sew each skirt piece, right sides together, to apron front at the waistline mark.

6. Finish sewing the 3" side edges of the apron front facing to the apron front. **Note:** *It may be easier to sew this section of the facing by hand.*

7. Zigzag stitch the edges of the seam allowance.

Add the Rickrack Hem

1. Sew a rickrack hem around the skirt edges. (See Rickrack Hem on page 11.)

Make the Ties

1. Fold ties lengthwise in half with right sides together. Sew along the long edge and across one short end. Trim off corner. Turn right side out and press. Topstitch close to edges.

2. Turn the open end of each tie strip ¼" to the back side. Press.

3. Pin the turned under end of one tie to the apron back at the top of the skirt approximately 1½" from the back edge, positioning ties with the seam side toward the bottom of the apron. Stitch along the folded edge and ⅜" from the folded edge. Repeat with the remaining tie on the opposite side of the apron.

4. Fold ties over the apron edge. Stitch along the edge of the enclosed seam allowance.

Add the Neck Straps

1. Iron a scrap of interfacing onto button and buttonhole placements of neck straps.

2. Pin the neck straps and neck strap facings right sides together. Stitch along the sides and around the curved end, leaving the straight edge open. Clip curves. Turn right side out and press. Topstitch close to edge.

3. Make two 1¼" buttonholes on one neck strap. Cut open.

4. Press raw edge of neck straps ½" toward the right side.

5. Pin neck straps to the wrong side at the top of the apron. Stitch-in-the-ditch from the front side to secure straps to apron. Hand-sew the bottom folded edge of the neck straps to the back of apron. (See Stitch-in-the-Ditch on page 15.)

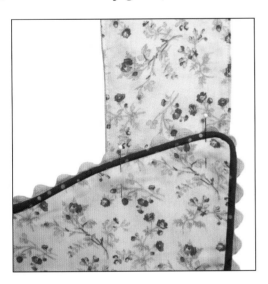

6. Try the apron on and pin neck straps together to make the best fit. Use pins to mark placement for your buttons. Sew buttons on.

My Apron Memory

It's fun reminiscing about my grandmother. She always wore some type of an apron, usually with pockets. She gathered eggs in the pockets and kept clothespins in them when hanging out her wash. She made jam, weeded her garden, and did all of her household chores with an apron on. One of my best memories is eating the foam that she skimmed off the cooked strawberry jam before she poured it into the jars.

Years later, I dropped a roll of 20 silver dollars into one of her apron pockets. She always thought my husband put them there, and I was glad it made her so happy!

Chris Jenkins
Henderson, Nevada

QUILTED PROJECTS
Chapter 4

YO-YO TABLE RUNNER

I wanted to include a table runner pattern in this book. I decided I would make it to match Minnie's Apron on page 18. I used extra prints from the same fabric line (designed by my friend, Brenda Pinnick) to make this runner. Have fun and mix up some of your favorite fabrics!

Finished Size
11½" x 44" (including yo-yos)

You will need
✳ 6 coordinating fat quarters for fabrics A–F
✳ ⅓ yard binding fabric
✳ 16" x 45" piece of backing fabric
✳ 16" x 45" piece of heat-resistant batting
✳ Thread to coordinate with fabrics
✳ Grip enhancer
✳ Temporary spray adhesive
✳ 1¾" yo-yo maker, optional
✳ Hand-sewing needle
✳ Heavy cardboard or template plastic
✳ Basic sewing supplies, rotary cutting tools, ¼" quilting foot, walking foot, and darning foot

Cutting Instructions
1. Assign a letter (A–F) to each fat quarter. Cut the following:
- (1) 9½" x 12" A rectangle
- (2) 5½" x 12" B rectangles
- (2) 1½" x 12" C strips
- (2) 4" x 12" D rectangles
- (2) 1½" x 12" E strips
- (2) 6" x 12" F rectangles

2. Prepare a pattern for the 4" circle given on the pullout pattern sheet, using the heavy cardboard or template plastic. From the remainder of the fat quarters, cut (14) 4" circles for yo-yos. **Note:** *If using the yo-yo maker, disregard this step and follow the manufacturer's instructions to cut yo-yo pieces.*

3. Cut (3) 2¼" x 42" strips from the binding fabric.

Sewing Instructions
Note: *Please read all instructions before beginning this project. All seams are ¼"; use a ¼" quilting foot for accurate seams.*

1. Sew the A–F strips and rectangles together on the 12" edges to make the runner top.

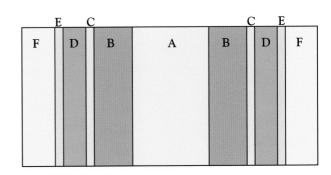

2. Press the seams away from the C and E strips. Press the remaining seams to one side.

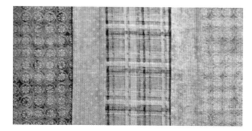

Quilt the Runner

1. Layer the backing (face down), batting, and runner top (face up). Apply temporary spray adhesive on both sides of the batting to hold layers together.

2. With your walking foot and the stitch-in-the-ditch method, sew along several of the seams to secure the runner. **Note:** *Use the same-color thread in the bobbin and the needle. (See Stitch-in-the-Ditch on page 15.)*

3. With your darning foot attached and feed dogs lowered, quilt a loopy pattern all over the runner. (See Quilting on page 13.)

4. Trim all edges even with the runner top in preparation for binding.

Add the Binding

1. Prepare binding using the 2¼" x 42" strips. (See Binding on page 14.)

2. Bind the edges of the runner.

Make the Yo-Yos

1. If you are using a yo-yo maker, prepare 14 yo-yos following the manufacturer's directions.

2. To make yo-yos without a yo-yo maker, thread the hand-sewing needle. Double the thread and make a knot at the end.

3. Sew a long gathering stitch around the edge of a 4" circle, turning the edge ¼" to the wrong side as you sew.

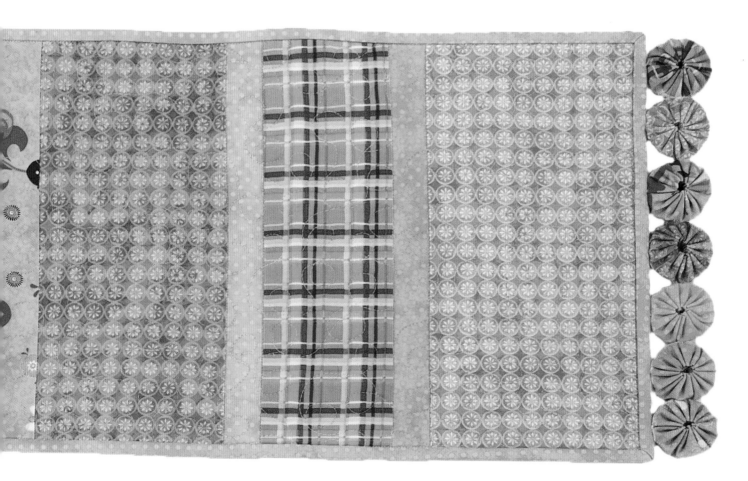

4. Pull the thread to tightly gather the circle. Knot and cut the thread. Flatten the circle with the gathered opening in the center of the top side to complete one yo-yo.

5. Repeat steps 2–4 to make a total of 14 yo-yos.

6. Evenly position seven yo-yos at each end of the runner. With the hand needle and matching thread, hand-tack the edge of each yo-yo to the edge of the runner. Hand-tack the yo-yos to each other. Gently press.

My Apron Memory

My mom had a clear plastic apron with red plastic trim around the edges and red plastic ties. I was elementary school age when I wore this apron. The red plastic edging was like a ruffle all around. The clear plastic had small raised bumps. I can picture it so well. She hung it in a closet off the kitchen where she kept the vacuum and other cleaning supplies. Any time we had spaghetti for dinner, which was pretty often, she had me get that apron out of the closet and tie it around my neck. I don't recall her, or anyone else in the family, ever wearing it.

I wish I had that apron now when I splatter my white shirt with spaghetti sauce! I will have to ask Mom if she remembers it. She seems to remember things from the past, so it will be interesting to see if she remembers this.

Judy Cooper
Bay Village, Ohio

RUFFLED PLACEMATS

These are the cutest placemats! I fell in love with this fabric and couldn't resist making more projects. I love the whimsy of the ruffles! Have fun and make these in different prints, to match all the aprons in this book. These can also be made without ruffles!

Finished size
11" x 17"

You will need (makes 2)
* ⅝ yard large floral fabric
* ¾ yard gingham fabric
* ¼ yard print fabric
* (2) 15" x 21" rectangles heat-resistant batting
* Thread to match fabrics
* Temporary spray adhesive
* Grip enhancer
* Basic sewing supplies, rotary cutting tools, ¼" quilting foot, and darning foot

Cutting Instructions
1. Cut (1) 6" x 42" strip from the large floral; recut into (4) 6" x 9" rectangles.
2. Cut (4) 2¼" x 42" strips from the large floral for binding.
3. Cut (1) 6" x 42" strip from the gingham; recut into (4) 6" x 9" rectangles.
4. Cut (2) 15" x 21" rectangles from the gingham for backings.
5. Cut (4) 2¼" x 21" strips from the print for ruffles.

Sewing Instructions
Note: Please read all instructions before beginning project. All seams are ¼".

1. Sew each large floral rectangle to a gingham rectangle on the 6" edges. Press seams toward the large floral rectangles. Sew two of the strips together. Press seam to one side to complete one placemat top. Repeat to make a second placemat top.

Quilt the Layers
1. Layer a backing rectangle (face down), batting, and placemat top (face up). Apply temporary spray adhesive on both sides of the batting to hold layers together. Repeat to make a second layered rectangle.
2. With your darning foot attached, feed dogs lowered and matching thread in bobbin and needle, machine quilt the placemats in a loopy design. (See Quilting on page 13.)
3. Trim all edges even with the placemat tops.

Add the Binding
1. Prepare binding using the 2¼" x 42" strips. (See Binding on page 14.)
2. Bind the edges of the placemats.

Add the Ruffles
1. Make a rolled hem or pressed rolled hem on each long side and both short ends of each ruffle strip. (See Hemming on page 11.)
2. Sew two rows of gathering stitches along the center of each ruffle. Gather to fit the ends of the placemats (approximately 11½"). (See Gathering on page 10.)
3. Position a ruffle just inside of the binding on the end of one placemat. Pin each end of the ruffle to the top and bottom edges of the placemat. Adjust gathers evenly along the length of the ruffle.
4. Sew along ruffle center, adjusting ruffles as you go, backstitching at the beginning and end.
5. Repeat to add a ruffle to each end of the placemats.

Ruffled Oven Mitts

After making the placemats, I knew I had to create some matching oven mitts! I love the fabric and how the mitts look with the ruffle. These can be made without the ruffle, too. But, the ruffle gives such an upbeat touch! You can easily change the look of these mitts by changing the fabric.

Finished Size
7½" x 12"

You will need (makes 2)
* ⅝ yard floral fabric
* ⅛ yard gingham fabric
* ⅝ yard lining fabric
* (2) 15" x 21" rectangles heat-resistant batting
* (2) 15" x 21" rectangles cotton batting
* Thread to match fabrics
* Temporary adhesive spray
* Grip enhancer
* Basic sewing supplies, rotary cutting tools, sharp scissors, ¼" quilting foot, and darning foot

Cutting Instructions
1. Cut (1) 12" x 42" strip from the floral; recut into (2) 12" x 18" rectangles.
2. Cut (1) 2¼" x 42" strip from the floral; recut into (2) 2¼" x 21" strips for ruffles.
3. Cut (1) 2¼" x 42" strip from the floral for binding.
4. Cut (1) 2¾" x 42" strip from the gingham; recut into (2) 2¾" x 18" strips.
5. Cut (1) 15" x 42" strip from the lining fabric; recut into (2) 15" x 21" lining rectangles.

Sewing & Quilting Instructions
Note: *Please read all instructions prior to making. All seams are ¼".*

1. Sew a 2¾" x 18" gingham strip to a 12" x 18" floral rectangle. Press seam open. Repeat.
2. Layer a lining rectangle (face down), cotton batting, heat-resistant batting, and one stitched section (face up). Apply temporary spray adhesive between the layers to hold together. Repeat to make a second layered rectangle.
3. With your darning foot attached, the feed dogs lowered and matching thread in the bobbin and needle, machine quilt the layered rectangles in a loopy design. (See Quilting on page 13.)
4. Trim the batting and lining even with the tops.

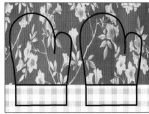

Prepare the Mitts
1. Prepare a tissue paper pattern for the Oven Mitt piece using the pattern given on the pullout pattern sheet.
2. Cut two mitts from one quilted section, aligning the seam between the gingham strip and floral rectangle with the line on the pattern. Flip the pattern over and cut two reversed mitts from the remaining quilted section.
3. Place a mitt and reversed mitt right sides together. Sew along the straight edge of the mitts. Stop stitching before you get to the curve. Repeat with the remaining mitt and reversed mitt.

Add the Binding
1. Prepare binding using the 2¼" x 42" floral binding strip. (See Binding on page 14.)
2. Bind the bottom edge of each mitt. Trim binding even with the side edges of the mitts.

Add the Ruffles
1. Make a rolled hem or pressed rolled hem along each 21" edge of the floral ruffle strips. (See Hemming on page 11.)
2. Sew two gathering stitches down center of each strip. Gather to measure 12½". (See Gathering on page 10.)
3. Pin a ruffle on the right side bottom edge of one mitt, matching the ends of the ruffle to the side edges of the mitt. The ruffle should extend below the bound edge of the mitt about ¼".
4. Sew down the ruffle center, adjusting ruffles as you go, backstitching at the beginning and end. Trim the ruffle even with the side edges of the mitt, if necessary.
5. Repeat to sew the ruffle on the second mitt.
6. Fold the mitt to position right sides together. Stitch around the remaining side and top edges. Clip at curves and at the thumb indentation. Zigzag stitch the seam allowance to secure the threads. Turn right side out. Press the ruffle slightly. Repeat to complete the second mitt.

77

CIRCLE OVEN MITTS

These are so cute and "sew" easy! I had enough fabric left over from Pearl's Apron (see page 36) to make this set. Be creative and mix and match other fabrics you have left over.

Finished Size
9" circle

You will need (makes 2)
* ⅜ yard floral fabric
* ⅔ yard coordinating fabric
* 4 (10") squares cotton batting
* 4 (10") squares heat-resistant batting
* Thread to match fabrics
* Temporary spray adhesive
* Grip enhancer
* Heavy cardboard or template plastic
* Basic sewing supplies, rotary cutting tools, ¼" quilting foot, walking foot, and darning foot

Cutting Instructions
1. Cut (1) 10" x 42" strip each from the floral fabric and coordinating fabric; recut into (4) 10" squares from each fabric

Make the Oven Mitts
1. Layer squares in this order: floral fabric (face down), cotton batting, heat-resistant batting, and co-ordinating fabric (face up). Apply temporary spray adhesive between the layers. Repeat to make three more layered squares.
2. Pin around the edges, if needed.
3. Machine quilt in desired pattern. I used a loopy design. (See Quilting on page 13.)
4. Prepare a template for the 9" circle given on the pullout pattern sheet, using the heavy cardboard or template plastic. Mark a circle onto each layered square.
5. Cut each quilted square into a 9" circle to make four circles.
6. Cut two circles in half to make four half-circles.

Add the Bias Binding
Note: *Refer to Binding on page 14 throughout the following steps.*

1. Create 150" bias binding from the coordinating fabric, cutting bias strips 2¼" wide.

2. Sew the binding on the straight edge of each half-circle. Trim ends even with the edges of the half-circles.

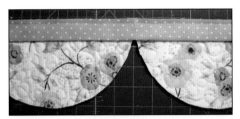

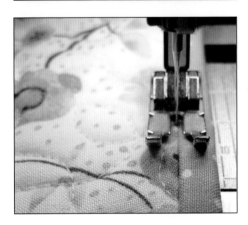

3. Position two half-circles on each circle with the coordinating fabric sides together. Pin to secure.
4. Baste around edges on both mitts. **Note:** *Use your walking foot to keep the layers from shifting.*
5. Bind the outer edges of each circle to complete the oven mitts.

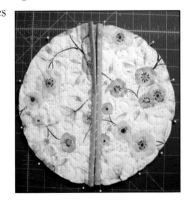

Denise Clason has been an artist/designer for over 35 years, selling her creative and beautiful designs to friends and teachers from an early age. Her designs have been published and licensed in the craft, decorative painting, sewing, and quilting industries.

Denise has written nine books, including *Sewing Vintage Aprons*. Her last two books were *New Country Quilting* and *Quilted Bags and Totes*. Denise designed and licensed two unique and creative fruit and quilt button lines called Stitchin' up the Pieces with JHB International.

Denise is a designer member of The Craft & Hobby Association. She loves to sew, quilt, garden, and create art. She has a married daughter, two grandchildren, and a son, who attends college out of state. Denise resides in Henderson, Nevada, with her husband. Please contact her at Denise@DeniseClason.com or visit her website, www.DeniseClason.com.

A special thank you to the owners and staff at Rose's Luncheonette, Route 46, Kenvil, New Jersey. They opened their restaurant to the photography staff from All American Crafts for a special photo shoot for Sewing Vintage Aprons. This was a perfect setting for the vintage aprons as the luncheonette dates back to the early 1930s. We would also like to thank Gail Nyez for coordinating the shoot with Rose's and with our models, Noelle DeMarco, Joanna Feller, and Taryn Torsiello.